If you are a teacher or any other category of human being who enjoys "putting the 'Active' in Activities" as Mariam MacGregor puts it, this book is for you . . . beautifully organized, created, and crafted.
—Gifted Education Communicator

A must-have for any teacher or advisor looking for new ways to motivate and instill vital leadership lessons.
—Laura Segura, executive director, National Teen Leadership Program

Association of Educational Publishers (AEP) Distinguished Achievement Award

Teambuilding
with Teens

Activities for Leadership, Decision Making, & Group Success

Mariam G. MacGregor, M.S.

free spirit
PUBLISHING®

Copyright © 2008 by Mariam G. MacGregor, M.S.

All rights reserved under International and Pan-American Copyright Conventions. Unless otherwise noted, no part of this book may be reproduced, stored in a retrieval system, or transmitted in any form or by any means, electronic, mechanical, photocopying, recording or otherwise, without express written permission of the publisher, except for brief quotations or critical reviews. For more information, go to www.freespirit.com/company/permissions.cfm.

Free Spirit, Free Spirit Publishing, and associated logos are trademarks and/or registered trademarks of Free Spirit Publishing Inc. A complete listing of our logos and trademarks is available at www.freespirit.com.

Library of Congress Cataloging-in-Publication Data
MacGregor, Mariam G.
    Teambuilding with teens : activities for leadership, decision making & group success / Mariam G. MacGregor.
       p. cm.
    Includes index.
    ISBN-13: 978-1-57542-265-7
    ISBN-10: 1-57542-265-4
    1. Group relations training. 2. Leadership—Study and teaching—Activity programs. 3. Teenagers. I. Title.
    HM1086.M33 2007
    302'.140712—dc22
                                                               2007028816

eBook ISBN: 978-1-57542-709-6

Free Spirit Publishing does not have control over or assume responsibility for author or third-party websites and their content. At the time of this book's publication, all facts and figures cited within are the most current available. All telephone numbers, addresses, and website URLs are accurate and active; all publications, organizations, websites, and other resources exist as described in this book; and all have been verified as of July 2011. If you find an error or believe that a resource listed here is not as described, please contact Free Spirit Publishing. Parents, teachers, and other adults: We strongly urge you to monitor children's use of the Internet.

The people depicted on the book cover are models and are used for illustrative purposes only.

Editor: Marjorie Lisovskis
Cover design: Percolator
Interior design: Percolator
Editorial assistant: Carla Valadez

10 9 8 7 6
Printed in the United States of America

Free Spirit Publishing Inc.
Minneapolis, MN
(612) 338-2068
help4kids@freespirit.com
www.freespirit.com

Printed on recycled paper
including 30%
post-consumer waste

As a member of the Green Press Initiative, Free Spirit Publishing is committed to the three Rs: Reduce, Reuse, Recycle. Whenever possible, we print our books on recycled paper containing a minimum of 30% post-consumer waste. At Free Spirit it's our goal to nurture not only children, but nature too!

Free Spirit offers competitive pricing.
Contact edsales@freespirit.com for pricing information on multiple quantity purchases.

DEDICATION

Dedicated to my husband and children, for modeling
the importance of leadership and teambuilding
at home, school, and all places in-between!

ACKNOWLEDGMENTS

Thank you to my editor, Margie Lisovskis, for her professionalism and high standards as we worked on this book, and to the other staff members at Free Spirit who contributed their time, energy, and expertise. A spirit of teamwork and group success was evident throughout the process.

Contents

List of Reproducible Forms vi
Introduction: Putting the "Active" in Activities 1

The Activities

Icebreakers **7**
Martian Names 8
Change the World 10
Handprints 12

Self-Awareness **14**
Body Map 15
Smirk 19
Becoming My Best 23
My Whole Self 30
Values Line 35

Working with Others **39**
Norms, Roles, and Expectations 40
House of Cards 45
Human Shuffle 48
The Mole 51
The Web 56

Communication **63**
Teams Building 64
Snowflake 67
Traveling Teams 69
Our Community 72
Puzzle 77

Qualities of Leadership **81**

Campaign Teams 82

Heroes 90

Treasure Hunt 93

The Party 98

Quote/End Quote 100

Wise Sayings 105

Social Issues **114**

Power Trip 115

Fruit Salad 120

Inside Out 124

Choosing Sides 128

Peace and Violence Webs 132

Decision Making and Problem Solving **137**

Bank Robbery 138

Community Action Plan 143

Challenges and Choices 148

Post Your Plans 156

The Million-Dollar Award 161

Closure **167**

Back/Feedback 168

Letter to Myself 170

Additional Resources **172**

What You Need to Conduct the Activities 173

Tips for Teens: Facilitating Group Activities 174

Overview of Learning Concepts and Activities 176

Correlations with *Building Everyday Leadership in All Teens* Curriculum 178

Index 181

About the Author 185

List of Reproducible Forms

Body Map Questions 17

Body Map Template 18

Becoming My Best: Who Supports Me? 26

Becoming My Best: What Inspires Me? 27

Becoming My Best: Who Supports Me?
(customizable) 28

Becoming My Best: What Inspires Me?
(customizable) 29

My Whole Self 33

The Whole Leader 34

Sample Words for Values Line 38

Norms, Roles, and Expectations 43–44

Team Instructions for Building a Card
Structure Replica 55

Special Mole Instructions 55

Web Key Words 59–60

Web Statements 61–62

Our Community 75

Our Community (customizable) 76

Puzzle Key 80

Profile of Candidate A 85

Profile of Candidate B 86

Profile of Candidate C 87

Profile of Candidate D 88

Profile of Candidate E 89

Treasure Hunt Questions 95–96

Treasure Hunt Score Sheet 97

Quotes 103

Quotes (customizable) 104

Wise Sayings 109–110

Wise Sayings (customizable) 111–112

Key to Wise Sayings 113

Power Trip Rules 118

Power Trip Team Tasks 119

Inside-Out Role Plays 127

Statements for Choosing Sides 131

Bank Robbery Clues 140–141

Bank Robbery Key 142

Community Action Plan 145–147

Ethical Choices Inventory 152–153

Ethical Choices Score Summaries 154

Creating a Group Code of Ethics 155

What Are Action Steps? 160

Profiles of Potential Award Winners . . 165–166

What You Need to Conduct the Activities . . 173

Tips for Teens: Facilitating
Group Activities 174–175

▰ INTRODUCTION ▰

Putting the "Active" in Activities

It's been shown that people, regardless of age, learn best by being immersed in experiences and by having chances to learn from firsthand circumstances. This principle is at the heart of *Teambuilding with Teens*, a compilation of activities that teach leadership, decision making, communication, and group dynamics. With the diversity of youth programs in many communities and the assorted ways schools address social development and group skills, educators and youth workers often find themselves pulling together activities from various sources. This book gathers, in a single volume, a broad collection of interactive activities that address a range of topics. It provides a complete resource to use in the classroom, in faith- and community-based organizations, at camps, in after-school activities, with athletic teams, or in any other setting where young people can explore character-building concepts.

The activities are ones I wrote or adapted specifically for use in classrooms or advisory groups where group members are working together to build their team. The words "Let's become a team!" aren't deliberately voiced. Instead, teens simply learn to enjoy working together and participating in lively learning experiences that make subject matter accessible and meaningful to them and that make sense in *their* here-and-now. Along the way, they develop strong leadership, communication, decision-making, and teamwork skills.

Experiential learning—learning by doing—jumpstarts creative thinking; it places teens into a simulated experience, provides opportunities for them to reflect on it, and encourages them to transfer what they learn to real life. Your class or meeting room will seem boisterous at times, but the noise level and movement can be indicators that teens are physically and mentally involved, embracing new ideas and acquiring new skills. At the same time,

conducting dynamic activities doesn't minimize the value of written work or in-depth projects. In fact, when students communicate and cooperate with one another, move around, and use their bodies in conjunction with their brains, their spoken and written expressions become more focused, thoughtful, and complete.

Using This Book in Your Setting

You can use *Teambuilding with Teens* in a wide variety of settings, in or out of school, including classrooms and after-school programs. The book is designed to be flexible. You may choose to conduct all the activities or select particular ones geared to a specific group focus. Depending upon your program goals and upon the participants you work with, you'll find useful activities for preservice or peer education training retreats. If you're a youth group leader, you'll also find activities you can use to help group members gain a better understanding of one another. An added benefit, especially if you're responsible for school-to-career preparation, is that all the activities emphasize an understanding of working with others—skills that will serve teens well throughout life.

You may want to use the book on its own or incorporate the activities into another curriculum or program. If you are already using a leadership curriculum, the activities in this book can serve as supplemental material. Often, groups latch on to a topic or need additional opportunities to experience and discuss it. Even with the organized delivery of a leadership curriculum, you may find that you need another lesson, want to explore certain topics more deeply or provide more opportunities for teens to develop skills, or have an extra day in the schedule. At these times, *Teambuilding with Teens* can be a ready support. (If you are using *Building Everyday Leadership in All Teens*, the chart on page 178 correlates that curriculum's sessions with activities in this book.)

Some youth programs take place once a month or during another designated time period. If you need occasional or ongoing activities to develop leadership skills over an evening meeting, a day-long workshop, a weekend retreat, or a month-long camp experience, this book provides diverse options to address specific topics. The activities are equally appropriate for students involved in student council, peer mentoring, and detention or probation programs. Finally, the activities are written so that experienced young people can conduct them as well, and after learning some basic facilitation skills (see pages 174–175), teen peer leaders will be confident conducting many of the exercises with other teens and, in some cases, with younger children.

Group Size

The ideal group size for conducting most of these activities depends on participants' ages, maturity, and experiences working with groups. For high school teens, a group of 16–25 typically works well; for middle school teens, a group of 12–18 is optimal. In either case, if the group is too small, the variety of perspectives that make learning more dynamic may not be as diverse; if the group is too large, everyone may not have an opportunity to share individual opinions or try new skills. If you are conducting the activities in a classroom with a larger group, you may want to divide teens into smaller groups that will simultaneously participate in an activity or, if appropriate, rotate teens to be observers. For activities where group size is critical, specific recommendations for adaptations are included.

Activity Sequence

The book begins with "Icebreakers" and ends with "Closure" activities. In between are activities organized into six topic areas: "Self-Awareness," "Working with Others," "Communication," "Qualities of Leadership," "Social Issues," and "Decision Making and Problem Solving." This sequence of topics is arbitrary, and you may use the book's activities in any order you wish.

If *Teambuilding with Teens* is your primary resource guide, you may want to begin with activities that allow teens to warm up as a group, learn values and attitudes that may impact how the group works together, and then move into activities that rely on greater self-disclosure and

address tougher issues or skills for the group to tackle. The topics you cover to accomplish this will depend on your group's particular purpose and needs.

Another approach is to focus on one particular topic before moving on to the next section of the book. In this case, you could work through all of the activities in one section, such as "Communication," before proceeding to a different section. Here, too, the activities in each section can be organized in any manner you prefer, taking into consideration your group rapport and specific issues facing the group at the time.

Many of the learning concepts overlap from section to section. For example, problem solving is addressed not only in activities under "Decision Making and Problem Solving" but in activities from other sections as well. Several concepts (such as personal values, teamwork, group dynamics, and communication skills) are a focus of various activities throughout the book. With this in mind, refer to the "Overview of Learning Concepts and Activities" chart (pages 176–177) if you wish to further organize activities around specific learning concepts.

Using the Activities

Activity Format

There is a common format for the activities, each of which is organized as follows:

- **Learning Concepts**—a list of the topics covered in the activity

- **Activity Preview**—a brief explanation of the activity and the estimated time it will take to conduct it, including time for discussion

- **Goals**—the purpose of the activity and what teens will learn or accomplish

- **Materials Needed**—what you'll need to conduct the activity

- **Getting Ready**—steps to prepare for conducting the activity; may include adaptations for group size, physical abilities, age level, or setting

- **Setting the Stage**—some activities include background information for you or the participants

- **Activity**—step-by-step guidance through the planned activity

- **Talk About It**—discussion questions to use with the group following the activity

- **Variation**—some activities include suggestions for further tailoring the activity to your group or for presenting it differently

- **Extending the Learning**—some activities include suggestions for extending or enhancing the lessons taught in the activity

- **Reproducible Forms**—some activities require reference sheets or student handouts, which are provided at the end of the activity

Getting Ready to Lead an Activity

Prior to conducting an activity, be sure to read through it to familiarize yourself with the goals and focus, check the sequence and timing, and review the background information and discussion questions.

The activities are written and designed with a minimum of required props, so you don't need to find obscure items in order to conduct each lesson. Many activities call for similar materials, and it can be efficient to collect these items in a box so you have a ready-to-use resource that you can keep close at hand and carry with you to any setting. You'll find a list of these standard activity materials ("What You Need to Conduct the Activities") on page 173. Beyond this collection, you will occasionally need additional materials for some activities. All required materials are listed at the beginning of each activity under "Materials Needed." Gather the materials ahead of time, making photocopies of forms or preparing charts or other props as directed in the "Getting Ready" section of the activity.

The length of time necessary to conduct the activities varies, in most cases ranging from approximately 20–45 minutes. This time frame allows you to incorporate the activities into your classroom period or group meeting schedule in a manner that best fits your objectives. It is important to always build in time for discussion so teens have the opportunity to understand how the activity applies to their daily lives. A few activities are best conducted over 45–60 minutes, and in some cases you may want to use more than one meeting time. These recommendations are stated at the beginning of the activity.

When background information is included ("Setting the Stage"), review this material. It will give you context for the activity or for skills and lessons teens will be learning. Make a note of any part of the information you wish to share with students.

Nearly all activities include a closing discussion ("Talk About It"). After you've conducted an activity once or twice, jot down any additional questions that you find useful for discussions or that relate specifically to the setting or teens you're working with. If you prefer, select one or two of the activity's discussion questions and assign these for written reflection.

Setting the Tone

It's essential to promote a safe environment that encourages supportive attitudes for and from everyone. Also, because the activities are interactive and often require moving with and around one another, you'll need to express your expectations about how to keep learning productive. Some teens are uncomfortable being physically close to peers, while others are at ease with lots of interaction. Remind teens that even though they are moving around the room for many of the activities, it's important that they stay on task within appropriate space boundaries inside the room and in relation to one another.

Understanding Groups

Years ago, Bruce W. Tuckman, Ph.D., a psychology professor at Ohio State University, researched and wrote about the developmental sequence of how small groups work together. His research findings have become benchmarks of the progression of group dynamics, and it's likely you'll see the sequence he identified in the groups of teens you work with, especially if your group is meeting or working together over time.[1]

Tuckman identified four stages of group dynamics—forming, storming, norming, and performing. He later added a fifth stage, adjourning, to describe when a group has no additional purpose for being together. Briefly, the first four stages are explained like this:

1. **Forming:** The group is just getting acquainted and will rely on the leader (facilitator) to guide them and determine group goals. Other than getting to know one another and finding out what people have in common, the group doesn't have a shared goal or purpose. An example is when a group of teens first enters your classroom or program, unaware of who the other members are or what their purpose is in being together.

2. **Storming:** The group has met before and now spends time trying to figure out how each person fits into

[1] A more in-depth explanation and application of Dr. Bruce Tuckman's stages of group development can be found in the original article "Developmental Sequence in Small Groups," *Psychological Bulletin* 63 (1965), 384–399, reprinted in *Group Facilitation: A Research and Applications Journal* 3 (Spring 2001). The article is available as a Word document at www.dennislearningcenter.osu.edu under "References."

the group. The atmosphere isn't nearly as friendly and inclusive as in the forming stage as people try to firm up roles, goals, and relationships within the group. Continuing the example from the first stage, during the storming stage some cliques may form as people begin to connect with those who share similar values or attitudes. The leader may still be heavily involved in providing guidance.

3. **Norming:** The group has met more often and established common goals and expectations of one another and the group. The group is able to make big decisions together and productively work through challenges. The atmosphere has become more sincere, sociable, and connected. The leader is more a consultant than the driving force. Following through with the example, the group has now participated in some activities or projects together, and teens are generally willing to share their opinions openly to help the group improve when working together.

4. **Performing:** The group has become a well-functioning team that shares a vision and goals. If disagreements arise, the team works cooperatively to resolve them. Although the team still expects the leader to tell them what needs to be accomplished or to point out tasks they may overlook, they don't need specific instructions. Now, focused on a mission such as a service project, they work together to make sure they achieve their individual and team goals within the group.

It's not unusual for adolescent groups to bounce back and forth among the first three stages before solidly reaching the performing stage. These fluctuations are affected by such things as a group being brand new or participants coming and going due to their schedules. The nature of adolescent relationships also affects a teen group's facility in moving beyond personal friendships or cliques on their way to creating inclusive, well-functioning teams. Therefore, if your group doesn't have an established mutual goal or vision (such as an after-school intervention program where students share an understood purpose), you'll want to create an atmosphere where teens identify common reasons for being there. The more personal these reasons, and the more readily group peers can relate to them, the greater will be your success in getting the group to work together on communication, leadership, and decision-making activities requiring more intense interaction.

With the four stages in mind, you'll begin to see familiar patterns in how teen groups work together as you conduct the activities in *Teambuilding with Teens.* To manage the earliest stage, conduct icebreakers, get-to-know-you exercises, and activities where you, the facilitator, guide the steps. As a group moves through the second and third stages, you can introduce more challenging topics and tasks. By the time groups reach the performing stage, you'll find they tend to successfully interact and cooperate with one another more readily. As a group nears the end of its overall time together, you'll want to conduct closure activities that are meaningful to individual participants as well as to the group as a whole.

Establishing Group Guidelines

From your group's onset, it is important to let participants know what to expect from you and from each other. You, your school, or your organization may have a general set of group guidelines in place. If you do, make these clear to the group at the beginning of your time together and make certain everyone understands and agrees to them. If there are no established guidelines, consider guiding the group to set their own with ideas like these:

• Members of the group listen to each other and treat one another with respect.

• Everyone is encouraged to share ideas although no one is required to do so.

• Everyone in the group should feel accepted and valued.

• All points of view are welcome.

The activity "Norms, Roles, and Expectations" (pages 40–44) focuses specifically on developing group guidelines and could be used in an early meeting with your group to set the tone.

Confidentiality

With your particular setting in mind, you may need to take into consideration confidentiality issues that arise during the discussion process of the activities. Where confidentiality is involved, remind teens of the importance of maintaining a group atmosphere that's respectful of diverse opinions. Instruct group members to honor everyone's confidentiality. Caution them not to mention other people's personal information or to use real names when recounting interactions or conflicts, both within or outside the group.

When conducting the activities, you may discover that some topics evoke personal admissions and highly charged situations. It's hard to predict exactly when someone may become emotionally affected or when conflict may arise within a group. But if you establish trust early on and monitor any particular dynamics among members, you likely will be able to anticipate potentially difficult circumstances. If intense moments occur, consider the stage the group is in, remind teens about maintaining confidentiality, and help those in disagreement to talk it through.

On rare occasions while discussing personal topics or challenging social issues, a teen may reveal private information. If a disclosure is troubling to you, talk with another adult decision maker or with your supervisor or principal. If a teen reveals that she or he is living in an abusive situation, you are obligated to report what you've heard. Follow the guidelines of your school or organization, or check with your principal or agency head about how to proceed.

Dealing with Difficult Discussions

Difficult discussions can arise for a variety of reasons: a topic may bring up anxiety for certain individuals, an activity may move some teens out of their comfort zone, or interactions between teens may become heated due to differences of opinions. It's wise to be prepared to help teens learn to navigate such situations.

If you suspect that a particular topic or activity may lead to difficult conversations or controversy, you can take preemptive steps to maintain a positive, productive learning environment. One step is to acknowledge at the start that the activity may challenge or upset some people and that the goal is to stay open-minded in order to learn as much as they can from it. Another is to set or remind teens of agreed-upon ground rules for the group, with an emphasis on tolerance and understanding different points of view.

Should you unexpectedly find teens in heated debate with each other, try to diffuse the situation by encouraging all parties to air opinions without judging or attempting to persuade those who don't share their perspective. Regardless of the subject matter that has sparked strong emotions, take time to draw on examples or situations that help the individuals connect personally to the existence of diverse viewpoints. If necessary, encourage teens to take a step back, think about how and why the activity is affecting them so dramatically, and spend some time talking about this. Point out the value of being able to express how one feels alongside the value of not having

views or opinions forced on someone by others; remind participants that these are important experiences for everyone in the group.

Skills Practice

Many of the activities depend upon one or more of the teens taking a leadership role or guiding the group process. Ask different volunteers to assume these roles for each activity, so everyone gets a chance to practice leadership and decision-making skills along with contributing to the group's development and success. (For purposes of this book, *leadership skills* broadly covers communication, ethical action, teamwork, tolerance, understanding values, problem solving, and several other dynamics. These skills are identified in the "Learning Concepts" highlighted at the beginning of each activity and in the "Overview of Learning Concepts and Activities" chart on pages 176–177.) At times, you may want to randomly pick participants' names out of a box or hat. Encourage reluctant teens to give it a try, and promote the activity as an opportunity rather than a requirement.

As the facilitator, you can help teens practice skills comfortably by providing participants plenty of opportunities to try new skills, looking for what's "right" in what teens are doing, and giving helpful, positive feedback. For teens who will call on their own experience as a participant when they are in the position of a facilitator, your feedback provides useful guidance in how to successfully conduct the activity themselves.

Some activities use role playing as the teaching technique. Role playing provides participants a fun opportunity to experience different perspectives in small or large groups. Teens assume the roles of certain characters and act out various scenarios. Although much of the role playing in the activity is scripted to support an expected outcome, you still need to address some basic ground rules for role playing. Remind participants that they don't have to reveal personal information in role playing, and encourage them to avoid acting overly silly or without focus. If this occurs, stop the role playing and remind students of its purpose. Role playing is most meaningful when participants and observers take time afterwards to discuss their reactions to the role play and its application to the everyday world.

As teens practice different leadership and group roles, their learning takes on a real-life aspect. This makes it easier to apply the lessons learned and identify strategies when actual situations arise in their daily activities. The activities are designed to be engaging and appealing, but there may still be some teens who participate minimally. By promoting and encouraging their role within the group and highlighting how what they learn applies in their personal lives, you can help them become more interested in improving their overall leadership and decision-making skills.

Encouraging Writing, Reflection, and Action

You may want to identify a method for teens to keep track of what they learn. This can be accomplished by having them keep a personal notebook or journal where they can write down thoughts after the activity. This also offers a place for participants to keep any handouts or other work they completed. Although each activity prompts you to do some sort of wrap-up, you may wish to carry this further. For example, you may want to have teens work toward creating a mural or service project together that connects what they learn through the activities. In this case, allow time for teens to work on the identified group project during the wrap-up time and then encourage writing in their journals between group meetings.

The Group That Works Together Succeeds Together

Every group of teens is different. The sports team that meets five times a week and plays a game on Saturdays varies in obvious ways from the youth group that meets once a month. But these differences don't prevent individuals from learning the skills that make them successful members of their group. By participating and learning from others in a group setting, teens are able to transfer their leadership, decision-making, and getting-along skills into real situations now and in the future. When teens are prepared to be strong group members—to actively fulfill their roles and responsibilities as part of a team—they are on their way to success as students, friends, employees, volunteers, and community leaders. Your guidance in this preparation is crucial, and there's no reason that a learning process with such a significant impact can't be lively and engaging for everyone involved.

Whether you're a seasoned teacher or group facilitator or you're new to working with a class or youth group, these activities were created with you in mind. Use them as they're written or add your own spin as you find what works best in your setting. Either way, enjoy inspiring teens with the long-lasting confidence and personal growth that comes from being part of a successful group.

Please contact me if you have any questions or experiences to share. You can reach me at:

Free Spirit Publishing Inc.
217 Fifth Avenue North, Suite 200
Minneapolis, MN 55401-1299
help4kids@freespirit.com

Mariam G. MacGregor, M.S.

Icebreakers

Martian Names

Change the World

Handprints

Martian Names

- Group warm-up • Getting to know others

(25–35 MINUTES)

This is a relatively low-risk icebreaker to get members of the group to introduce themselves in a creative manner. Teens write their names backward (in "Martian language") and then explain to the group what they mean. This light approach helps participants feel comfortable sharing a little about themselves. The activity is effective with groups of all ages, easy and fun to conduct at the first meeting, and useful in establishing a positive and warm group atmosphere.

GOALS

Participants will:

- introduce themselves to one another
- learn names of others in the group
- share something about themselves

MATERIALS NEEDED

- Markers
- 8½" x 11" colored paper

GETTING READY

To assist with explaining the activity, it's helpful if you have created your own "Martian name" sheet ahead of time and have determined what your name means in Martian language.

Activity

Pass out a piece of paper and marker to each participant. Create and tell a story to set up the activity, such as this:

Imagine you have just landed on Mars and need to introduce yourself to your Martian tour guide. Language on Mars is the complete reverse of ours. This means you must change your name so it's backward:

last name first, first name last, and both spelled backward, letter by letter. In addition, every name on Mars means something special and relates to the person who has that name. For example, my Martian name is _____,
which means _____.
(Hold up the name sheet that you prepared prior to conducting the activity.) **On your sheet of paper, write your name as it would appear on Mars. Practice pronouncing it. Think about what your Martian name means and be prepared to share it with everyone in the group.**

While participants are deciding what their names mean, encourage them to consider things that are important to them—special quotes, something they are good at, unique personal characteristics, cultural values, or other interests. This can assist them in creatively sharing information about themselves without necessarily risking too much in an early-forming group. Here are some examples:

- Sarah Jones becomes "Senoj Haras," which means "enjoys taking long trips and hiking with my friends."

- Javier Martinez becomes "Zenitram Reivaj," which means "a very loyal friend and a good son."

Talk About It

When all students have finished writing their names, go around the group and, one at a time, have participants hold up their name sign, introduce themselves, and explain what their name means. In addition, have teens introduce their actual (Earth) names and say one or two other things about themselves if they wish. You may also choose to ask each participant to respond to questions such as these:

- **Why are you participating in this (class, camp, club, workshop, group)?**

- **What do you hope to gain from participating?**

- **What are you hoping to contribute to the group?**

- **What is one of your favorite topics for discussion?**

Wrapping Up

At the end of the activity, and if space allows, hang the sheets up on a bulletin board or wall and leave them there for a few meetings to keep the group atmosphere friendly and warm. Otherwise, allow teens to take the name sheets home.

Change the World

LEARNING CONCEPTS

- Getting to know others • Vision and values
- Critical thinking and social change

(45 MINUTES)

For this activity, teens respond to a question prompt to create posters that express, visually and verbally, what the world would look like if they could change it. It is a simple yet powerful way to get teens talking about their community, the world around them, and their roles within a social system. This is a good group-introduction activity; it is also useful when teens are preparing to be involved in community service or advocacy efforts.

GOALS

Participants will:

- introduce themselves to the group
- gain awareness of topics or issues that are important to others in the group
- establish an understanding of what is valued by peers in the group

MATERIALS NEEDED

- Markers, colored pencils, or crayons
- 9" x 12" or 12" x 18" construction or drawing paper

GETTING READY

Place the paper, markers, pencils, and crayons in an area easily accessible to everyone in the group as they work on their posters.

Activity

Have teens select a piece of paper and several markers, pencils, or crayons. Then ask them to find a comfortable spot where they can think and draw on the paper. Explain the activity by saying:

On your sheet of paper, you'll create a poster by drawing a picture or an image, or by writing a quote or statement, in response to this question:

• If you could change the world, what would it look like?

Your poster does not have to be particularly artistic. Simply think about what changes you would want in the world if you had the power to make them happen. Maybe you'd like to see a cure for a certain disease or the end of certain social troubles; your changes might affect millions or they might make a smaller impact. Create your poster with that in mind. You have 10 minutes.

Depending on the level of abstract or critical thinking skills of your group, you may need to help participants get started. Walk around the room to guide teens in their efforts and, if necessary, ask brief questions to help focus and clarify what they want to change. Encourage students to use metaphors, quotes, poetry, symbols, drawings, colors, and other methods to express their perspectives.

Once everyone has completed a poster, bring the group back together and have each person share his or her work with the entire group. Provide an opportunity for teens to ask one another questions; encourage them to do so. You may want to ask your own brief questions to further assist participants in expressing what they've drawn on their paper. Depending on the size of your group, this sharing can take 20–30 minutes. If you are using this as an introduction exercise, provide enough time for individual students to present plenty of explanation or background about their posters.

VARIATIONS

If the activity is used after teens have established rapport, you may choose to revise or expand the question prompt to address specific topics your group is working on or discussing. For example, if the group is preparing to undertake a service project, you could phrase the question like this: "By the time your group finishes your service project, what impact do you hope to leave on the people you're serving? What kind of difference do you want to make for them?" Or for more global topics, you might phrase it: "If you were able to make a difference in the lives of people living in war or poverty, what would that difference look like? You can also show what it would look like if world leaders worked to make a long-lasting difference."

If you're conducting this activity as part of a career-preparation program, you could use a prompt like this: "Think about your dream job. What does it look like? What would you be doing? As you work toward your career, what do you need to do to be prepared for your dream job? What changes do you need to make in your life to get ready?"

Talk About It

Use 5–10 minutes to have teens talk about their thoughts during the activity. Ask these discussion questions related to your group's experience:

• What was it like to be asked this question? What were the first images or ideas that came to mind?

• How do you feel you can influence the future, both as an individual and as part of a group?

• What role do you think people have in creating the future you envision on your poster?

• What do you think you would hear if you asked this same question of others who are older or younger than you?

Wrapping Up

At the end of the activity, and if space allows, hang the posters around the room or in a more visible hallway so others can look at, read, and think about them. If space doesn't allow this, let teens take their posters home.

Handprints

LEARNING CONCEPTS

- Recognizing role models • Group warm-up or closure
- Getting to know others • Personal values

(20–25 MINUTES)

This activity encourages participants to think about people who have touched their lives in positive and influential ways. Teens trace their handprints, write (in the fingers) names of role models who demonstrate certain qualities or behaviors, and share what they wrote with the group. Used as an icebreaker, the activity allows others a peek into the people individuals value in their lives and sets a tone for achieving certain leadership or character goals. A variation provides qualities and questions to consider if using the exercise for group closure.

GOALS

Participants will:
- identify how people positively influence their lives
- share insight into who and what they value
- set a warm tone for a new group or allow for appreciations during group closure

MATERIALS NEEDED

- Newsprint
- Masking tape
- Construction paper
- Markers or crayons
- *Optional*—Scissors, hole punch, yarn or twine

GETTING READY

Draw a large hand on a piece of newsprint, filling the sheet. Number the fingers 1–5, with the thumb being number 1 and the pinky finger 5. Within the fingers, write these five statements:

1. The person you most admire
2. Someone in life you think you can learn a lot from
3. Someone you know who has great leadership potential
4. The person in this group you are most looking forward to getting to know
5. The leadership trait or personality characteristic you most want people to use to describe you

12

Hang the newsprint hand in a visible location for teens to refer to when doing their handprints. Place the construction paper and markers or crayons in an area easily accessible to all.

VARIATION

If using this activity for closure, write these statements in the fingers:

1. The person in this group you most admire
2. Someone in this group who has made the greatest impact on you
3. A person in this group you hope to work with again
4. A person in this group you enjoyed getting to know or think you could still learn a lot from
5. The leadership trait or personality characteristic you most want people to use to describe you

Activity

Invite teens to select a piece of paper and a marker or crayon and write their name at the top of their paper. Ask them to place one hand on the paper and trace the outline of that hand, spacing their fingers apart so that each one is clearly separated from the others.

Starting with the thumb, have participants label the fingers with the numbers 1–5 in exactly the same configuration shown on the sample poster. (This is for consistency as they share what they've written in each finger.) Explain the reason a handprint is used for this activity by saying:

In your life, there are people who have touched you in meaningful ways. Although you aren't always aware of their touch when it happens, you recognize it when given a chance to think about it. Just as your handprints remain on the things you touch, so do other people's imprints remain with you.

In the individual fingers of their handprint, ask teens to write responses to the statements on the newsprint. Allow 5–10 minutes for people to do this. Once everyone has completed filling in the hands, bring the group together to share and discuss the handprints.

Talk About It

Use 10–15 minutes to have the group discuss the people and ideas evoked in the handprints. Depending on the rapport of the group, you may ask them to mention a few or all of the people they wrote down and briefly explain why they included particular individuals. During discussion time, encourage teens to ask their own questions about what people have written. In addition, discuss questions such as these:

- **When people impact your life in a positive way, how do you let them know it?**
- **What similarities are there among the people who've impacted your lives?**
- **How would you like others to think of your impact on *their* lives?**
- **What makes a person's impact most memorable?**

VARIATION

If using the activity for closure, you may want to ask:

- **If we hadn't done this activity, how would you have expressed your appreciation to people in this group who impacted you?**
- **Even though the group won't be meeting together any longer, how can you continue to positively influence each other?**
- **What steps will you take to make a positive impact on the lives of others beyond this group?**

Wrapping Up

If time allows, have teens cut out their hand tracings. Punch a hole in both the thumb and pinkie finger of each hand. Cut a piece of yarn or twine that's long enough to weave through the holes of all the hands to create a garland of handprints to display. Have teens work together to weave their hands onto the string and hang the completed garland along a wall or across the room. If space or time doesn't allow for this, encourage teens to put the handprints in their journals or notebooks for future reference.

Self-Awareness

Body Map

Smirk

Becoming My Best

My Whole Self

Values Line

Body Map

LEARNING CONCEPTS

- Self-awareness • Group development • Understanding others

(45 MINUTES OR MORE)

This activity gives teens an opportunity to visually express the qualities that make them unique and the outlook they bring to the group. With the help of a partner, they'll create a blank outline of their body. Then, in response to prompting questions, they'll individually fill in their body outlines with responses to the questions using pictures, symbols, quotes, phrases, and so forth. The activity typically results in a lot of sharing. For this reason, it is best used after your group has had a chance to get to know each other, even just a little. Time permitting, you may want to allot two meeting periods.

GOALS

Participants will:

- share their abilities and skills with others
- gain awareness of what others bring to the group
- recognize and appreciate individual group members' interests, expectations, and communication styles

MATERIALS NEEDED

- Markers or crayons
- Banner paper
- Scissors
- Masking tape
- Handout: "Body Map Questions" (page 17)

- *Optional*—Handout: "Body Map Template" (page 18), 17" x 22" copier paper

GETTING READY

Depending upon the size of your group and the time you have available, allot two 45-minute meetings for this activity—one to complete the body maps and the other for everyone to share and discuss what they depicted. Scheduling two meeting times prevents participants from feeling rushed through either part and encourages others in the group to ask questions of their peers.

Prior to meeting with the group, write the "Body Map Questions" (page 17) on the board or on a large sheet of banner paper. Hang the paper where all participants will be able to read it. Posting the questions, rather than simply reading them aloud, helps visual learners understand what is being asked and allows individual students to move at their own pace. If you prefer, make copies of the "Body Map Questions" handout and give one to each pair of teens to share as they work on their body maps.

Cut sheets of banner paper large enough for body tracing, one sheet per teen; gather enough markers or crayons for all participants.

If you have a limited area, you may choose to have teens create smaller body maps. If so, photocopy the "Body Map Template" handout for all participants to use instead of the larger banner paper. With this option, make copies on 17" x 22"

paper (set the copy ratio at 200%) to allow sufficient space for writing.

ACCOMMODATIONS

If your group has teens with limited physical mobility, getting on the ground for body tracing may be difficult or impossible. In these cases, have a partner or helper draw an outline that reflects the proportional size of the person—with or without wheelchair or other assisting device—if the teen agrees to this. You may also choose to use the "Body Map Template" handout rather than banner paper.

Activity

With students working in pairs, have each person trace the partner's outline on a large sheet of banner paper. (There is no need for participants to touch one another; if necessary, remind teens to maintain respectful boundaries.) While they are being traced, encourage students to lie with their arms and legs clearly identifiable. This creates a body map with larger areas to write or draw in when responding to the "Body Map Questions." This should take about 5 minutes.

Once everyone's outline is complete, ask students to look at and read the posted questions. Then say:

Starting from the top of your body map, write words or draw pictures or symbols that express your response to each question. Write or draw each response in the area of the body map that the question refers to. For example, for the questions next to the word "Brain" you'll write or draw your responses on the head.

Encourage students who are drawing pictures to use symbols that everyone in the group will understand. Tell teens they will have 25 minutes to complete their body maps.

Talk About It

When the body maps are completed, bring the group together and use the remaining 15 minutes to share and discuss what each person has expressed. As each teen presents his or her body map, tape it to the wall so everyone can see it as the person explains it. As teens

describe and share what they have written or drawn, encourage the group to ask questions. Also take time to conduct the discussion questions that follow. If your group is large, you may need additional time to complete this part of the activity. Or, you may want to divide your group into smaller groups of two or three and have the small groups share their body maps with one another before bringing the group together as a whole to discuss questions like these related to your group's experience:

- **Was this activity difficult or easy to do? What made it difficult (or easy)?**

- **As a group, how can you use what you've learned about each other? How will this information help you work as a team and develop your individual leadership skills?**

- **So that others in the group can better understand your personality or ways you can contribute, what else would you like to share about yourself that you didn't include on your body map?**

- **How does your body map relate to the goals you have as a leader? As a member of this team? As a member of other groups you're part of?**

Wrapping Up

At the end of the session, and if space allows, hang all the maps around the room so others can view and read them when the group gathers again. If space doesn't allow, teens may take the body maps home.

Body Map Questions

On your body map, write words or draw symbols that express your response to each of the following questions. Write or draw each response in the area of the body map that the question refers to. For example, for the questions next to the word "Brain," write or draw on the head; for "Skin" questions, use the area around the outline of the body.

Brain:

How do I remember information? What's the best way for people to give me messages that I'll remember?

What topics do I really like talking or learning about?

Eyes:

When people first meet or see me, what do I want them to learn about me?

What is a talent I have that others may not be aware of?

Mouth:

When or where am I comfortable expressing my beliefs, ideas, or feelings? What helps me feel comfortable doing this?

How do I communicate my opinions?

Ears:

How do I prefer to have people tell me things or give me constructive criticism?

How do I respond when others give me feedback I don't agree with?

If my life were a song, what song would it be?

Hands:

In what ways do I enjoy helping others?

In what ways do I sometimes need help from others (although I may not ask)?

Heart:

The things I value most (such as people, places, or beliefs) are . . .

If something has upset me, how do I respond and how do I want others to treat me?

The most rewarding experience I've had in my life so far is . . .

Legs:

What issues are important to me? What do I want to stand up and work for?

If I could take a trip (away from places I know best), where would my legs go?

Feet:

What tasks or hobbies do I eagerly do and jump into with both feet?

What tasks do I dislike doing and prefer to walk away from?

Skin:

What keeps me going when I'm feeling down?

What stresses me out? How do I deal with stress and stressful situations?

How do I make decisions? Do I rely on my heart, gut, head? Something else?

From *Teambuilding with Teens: Activities for Leadership, Decision Making, and Group Success* by Mariam G. MacGregor, M.S., copyright © 2008. Free Spirit Publishing Inc., Minneapolis, MN; www.freespirit.com. This page may be photocopied for individual, classroom, and group work only. For all other uses, call 800-735-7323.

Body Map Template

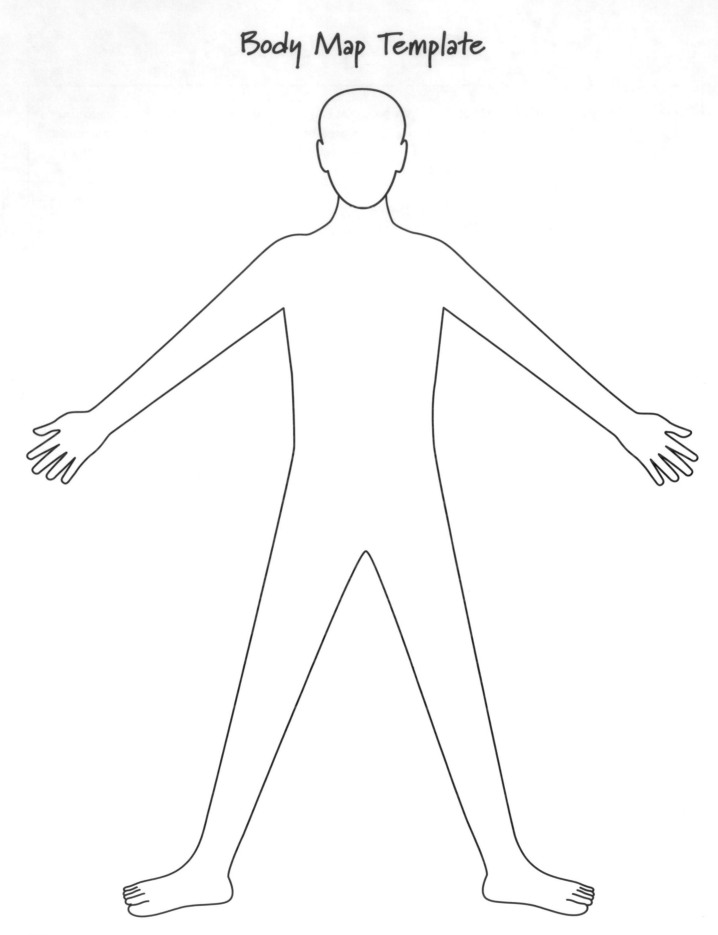

From *Teambuilding with Teens: Activities for Leadership, Decision Making, and Group Success* by Mariam G. MacGregor, M.S., copyright © 2008. Free Spirit Publishing Inc., Minneapolis, MN; www.freespirit.com. This page may be photocopied for individual, classroom, and group work only. For all other uses, call 800-735-7323.

Smirk

LEARNING CONCEPTS

- Moral independence • Positive versus negative peer pressure
- Teamwork and group dynamics

(35 MINUTES)

In this activity, teams compete to gain members by trying to get the opposing team to smile or laugh. A humorous way to challenge the ability of individual teen leaders to stand their ground, the exercise also requires strength as a team. Although the activity is simple, the process and the discussion that follows allow you to address challenging real-life situations. In addition to creating peer pressure, "Smirk" plays on how well a team works together to influence members of the opposing team. Even though individual participants want to be strong for their team, they are reminded that independent thinking can be very difficult. You will need ample space to set up teams in two lines, with room between the lines for two individuals to walk.

GOALS

Participants will:

- recognize the strength of both positive and negative peer pressure
- learn to work as a team in spite of other pressures
- clarify challenges that can arise even with an obvious group goal in mind

MATERIALS NEEDED

- *Optional*—Joke book (see "Variation"); pens, loose-leaf paper, and banner paper (see "Extending the Learning")

GETTING READY

Depending on the space you are using to conduct this activity, move any tables, chairs, or desks out of the way to create an open area for movement. Also, be prepared with a method of dividing your larger group into two smaller teams without allowing participants to select their own teammates.

ACCOMMODATIONS

For groups where teens have physical challenges requiring crutches or a wheelchair, this activity can still be conducted as described; it may require a larger space for movement. For physical challenges that limit eyesight, see the variation on page 21.

Setting the Stage

Even though this activity is simple on the surface, its lessons go deeper than convincing an opposing team's members to smile. After the activity has taken place, you'll want to spend some time talking about peer pressure and its influence on individuals and groups. Having the discussion before the activity gives away some of its impact, so consider including this topic as part of the "Talk About It" process.

With younger teens and preteens, the discussion can revolve around positive and negative peer pressure. *Positive peer pressure* is when group members or individuals are able to persuade others around them to do things that have positive outcomes (such as participating in service projects, striving to get good grades, or refraining from littering). *Negative peer pressure* is when group members or individuals persuade others around them to do things that have negative outcomes (such as joining a gang, drinking and driving, cheating, or skipping school).

Older teens may feel that they readily resist peer pressure and so the topic may seem juvenile to them. In this case, you may want to focus on the concepts of *groupthink* and *moral independence*. Consider these definitions to frame the activity and subsequent discussions:

Groupthink: This occurs when members of a group begin thinking alike to the point that they may not consider other alternatives for their situation or decision. Groupthink can be interpreted in the positive as consensus and overall agreement. It can also become negative when groups overlook making sound or safe decisions because they have started thinking very narrowly or have begun valuing the opinions and guidance of a select few. In these cases, group members may exert tremendous pressure on others in order to get them to agree with a certain decision or outcome.

Moral independence: This is present when members of a group are still fully capable of acting as individuals even in the context of highly pressured group situations. Acting with moral independence means one is able to live by what is true, even if others, even the whole group, stand opposed. Moral independence is exhibited when others are trying to convince someone to do something that is not consistent with the person's beliefs, and the person stands firm for what she or he believes is right.

"Extending the Learning" (pages 21–22) addresses understanding types of peer pressure, confronting negative peer pressure, and exploring ways to engage in positive peer pressure.

Activity

There are two parts to this activity. For the first part, you give instructions and the teams and individuals proceed with no additional discussion or planning. For the second part, the teams repeat this activity, this time taking a few minutes to strategize. You will discuss what happens after the group has completed both parts of the activity.

Divide the entire group into two teams. Do not allow them to select their team members; count off or use some other neutral mechanism for creating the teams. Have teams stand in parallel lines, with each line facing the opposing team. Allow enough space so two teens can walk side by side between the two lines without touching each other or anyone in the lines. Explain the goal of the activity by saying:

> **Each line is a team. As a team, you're going to try to get all of your team members to walk from one end of your line to the other. Two people—one from each team—will walk between the two lines at the same time. Everyone will take a turn. Sound easy? The catch is you need to get from the start to the finish without smiling. If you make it to the finish without smiling, you get to stay on your team. If you smile before finishing, the other team gets to add you to their line.**
>
> **Those of you on the sidelines can do what you want to get the walkers to smile, as long as you do *not* touch them or create any dangerous or awkward situations for either of them. The goal is to keep all the team members you started with and add as many as you can from the other side. I will let you know when each turn starts.**

Since teens will be trying creative ways to get others to smile, you may want to explain what sorts of things are appropriate. Encourage teens to use silly faces, non-offensive gestures, and funny sounds or movements and to tell jokes or riddles that the entire group will find funny. If the whole group starts laughing, it's quite difficult for the two walking down the middle not to find humor in the joke!

Set guidelines about making demeaning comments that one person may think funny but the receiver may find offensive. Also, discourage individuals from making comments that relate to inside jokes, since others in the group may infer that such jokes involve them. If teens in your group speak multiple languages, remind them that if they use a language unfamiliar to others in the group, they must still maintain decorum in their comments.

After explaining the rules, identify the starting and ending points. Ask the first person from each line to step to the middle of the two lines at the starting point. When you say "Go," the first pair begins walking down the line. Keep an eye out to make sure the pathway remains safe. Once they've made it to the end, have them rejoin their team or move to the other one, depending on whether either person smiled.

When everyone has passed through the line the first time, reassign them to their original teams. Then say:

Now that you've made it through, you will have another chance to increase your team numbers. This time, before sending members down the line, you will have 5 minutes to strategize as a team. When that time is up, you will once again line up and take turns walking in pairs from the start to the finish, trying not to smile before you reach the end.

Allow 5 minutes for team strategizing and then conduct the process as before. When everyone has gone through the lines, count the team members and declare the winning team. Depending on the size of your group, completing both parts of the activity, including strategizing, can take 20–25 minutes.

VARIATION

This activity can also be conducted by creating two lines seated on opposite sides of a table. Using a joke book or another funny resource, each line can pass a joke to the person whose turn it is to go down the line. The goal is the same—to get the individual to smile or laugh. This can work with a rectangular or circular table. As each opposing pair's turn comes up, they step forward to receive their joke from the other team.

Talk About It

Bring everyone together and take 10 minutes to talk about the entire activity, including the differences between having and not having time to strategize. In your discussion, be sure to talk about the ways strategizing takes place when there is peer pressure in everyday life. You may want to ask your group to give examples where such

strategizing has occurred in their own groups of friends. If necessary, share an example, such as when two people plan to persuade others in their group to agree to certain activities or ideas.

Consider these discussion questions related to your group's experience:

- **What was it like when it was your turn to walk between the lines?**

- **What did your team do to help each individual make it through to the other end? Did your team ever seem more focused on making the other team's members smile than they were in helping your own team members be successful? Explain.**

- **How did you feel, as an individual, when you couldn't make it to the other end without smiling? How did you feel as a member of your team? How did it feel to make one of the walkers smile?**

- **How was the experience different when your team was able to strategize? How was it the same? What were some strategies you came up with? Did everyone agree to all the strategies? Were there any ideas that made you uncomfortable? Explain.**

- **How does this activity relate to personal situations where others are pressuring you to do something you may or may not agree with or want to do? How do you help keep yourself focused on what's important to you so you can stand up for what you feel is right?**

Wrapping Up

After talking about the activity, encourage teens to take some time outside the group to observe their role in situations involving peer pressure. Encourage them also to notice how they react to or are influenced by peer pressure, both positive and negative. If time allows at the next group meeting, ask teens to share what they observed about themselves, their roles, and the pull of peer pressure in their lives. If you won't be able to have a conversation about this, ask teens to write their observations and thoughts in their journals or notebooks.

Extending the Learning

Explore peer pressure's pros and cons. Depending on your group, you may want to segue into a discussion about peer pressure. To further apply the learning, divide the group into smaller groups of three or four. Pass out a piece of loose-leaf paper and pen to each group; ask teens to write the heading "Positive" on one side of the paper and "Negative" on the other. In the small groups, ask teens to brainstorm examples of positive and negative peer pressure, writing their comments on the appropriate side. Then ask groups to share their examples. You may want to have a volunteer write the entire list on a chalkboard or large piece of banner paper. With the lists in front of the large group, conduct a discussion that addresses ways teens can appropriately manage negative peer pressure situations and ways they can engage in positive peer pressure.

Examine peer pressure in the larger world. For more mature groups, take time to introduce the terms *groupthink* and *moral independence* and have teens brainstorm examples of each. In this case, you will want them to think historically and globally so they can consider issues such as war, oppression of groups or individuals, substance use and abuse, gang recruitment and activity, cults, and other situations where peer pressure plays a positive or negative role.

Becoming My Best

LEARNING CONCEPTS

- Self-awareness • Personal values
- Balance and healthy life influences

(35–45 MINUTES)

Teens work independently to complete handouts, listing people and activities that support them in becoming their best selves. They then share what they have written with others in large or small groups. For some teens, this activity may be the first time they've sat down to think about what makes them happy in their lives and how this connects to their personal values. It can also inspire them to consider changing negative relationships or activities because they do not contribute to the growth they want for themselves. The activity promotes positive discussion, self-knowledge, and a greater awareness of making healthy life choices.

GOALS

Participants will:

- reflect on who and what is important in their lives
- gain awareness of who and what influences peers in the group
- identify healthy influences in their lives

MATERIALS NEEDED

- Pen or pencil for each participant

- Handouts: "Becoming My Best: Who Supports Me?" and "Becoming My Best: What Inspires Me?" (pages 26–27)
- *Optional*—Handouts: Customizable "Becoming My Best: Who Supports Me?" and "Becoming My Best: What Inspires Me?" forms (pages 28–29; see "Variation")

GETTING READY

Prior to your meeting time, make a copy of "Becoming My Best: Who Supports Me?" and "Becoming My Best:

What Inspires Me?" for each teen, copying them on one sheet of paper using both sides. Have pens or pencils available. Organize the room so that teens will have private space to complete their handouts before gathering in a large group (or small ones) later in the activity.

The statements on the handouts can be changed or adapted to better fit the youth population you work with. If you wish to create your own statements, use the customizable reproducible forms on pages 28–29. Write your statements on one copy and then make two-sided photocopies to distribute.

Setting the Stage

Since 1965, William Glasser, M.D., has practiced, written about, and taught a counseling technique called Reality Therapy. More recently, it has come to be based on Choice Theory, also formulated by Dr. Glasser. In Choice Theory, the goal of improving life situations is rooted in answering the driving question, "Is what I am doing getting me closer to the people I need?" If the answer is no, the goal is to make different choices that will improve the quality and positive nature of the relationships.

In its simplest form, the premise of Reality Therapy is that people are happiest and most successful when they look at choices and relationships in their life in *present* context. Reality Therapy doesn't consider past relationships as a basis for change; instead, it encourages individuals to reflect on, repair, or sever negative relationships in their lives. Its focus is on (1) looking at things that *can* be changed—thoughts and actions—as the basis for making positive choices and changes in life and (2) refraining from attempts to change things that *can't* be changed—feelings and physiological responses.

For this activity, participants will first look at the people in their lives who help them become their best by fulfilling their need for love and belonging, achievement, fun, and freedom. Teens will then consider the activities they choose to be involved in, evaluating them to determine if these choices fulfill the same four needs.

Apart from a focus on the importance of making choices—whether in relationships, leisure activities, or other personal arenas—teens do not need an explanation of Glasser's theories in order to benefit from the activity. And although it is based on these theories, it isn't necessarily a counseling or therapeutic exercise. With this in mind, you don't need to frame it as therapeutic, particularly if doing so will inhibit or dissuade some participants from reflecting on making positive changes in their lives.

If you are interested in further exploring these theories and their application in various settings, you may want to refer to one or more of these books:

Counseling with Choice Theory: The New Reality Therapy by William Glasser, M.D. (New York: Harper Paperbacks, 2001)

The Quality School: Managing Students Without Coercion by William Glasser, M.D. (New York: Harper Paperbacks, 1998)

Reality Therapy for the 21st Century by Robe Wubbolding (Philadelphia: Routledge, 2000)

Unhappy Teenagers: A Way for Parents and Teachers to Reach Them by William Glasser, M.D. (New York: HarperCollins, 2002)

Activity

Pass out the "Becoming My Best" handouts to each teen and explain the activity like this:

> **You are going to find a private place to write your responses to the statements on each side of this handout. I want you to think about the ideas as they relate to your life and the important people and activities in your life. You can think broadly for each section of the handout, or if you wish, you can narrow down your choices by thinking only of people and activities related to school or a favorite group you're part of. Please don't talk with others or share your responses until everyone has finished the sheet. You'll come back together as a group to discuss what you've written.**

It will take about 10–15 minutes for everyone to thoughtfully finish both sides of the sheet. When everyone has done this, bring the group together. Use 20–25 minutes to have teens share their responses to each quadrant on the form. This requires personal risk taking; remind group members to be respectful as they listen to what individual participants are saying. Depending on the nature and maturity of your group, you may want to encourage teens to ask appropriate and inquisitive questions of their peers as they share.

If your group is newly formed or if members are hesitant to speak, you may want to divide the larger group into smaller groups of three or four teens so they can share with a smaller audience. If some teens are familiar with others, try to split them up so they are in groups with people they may not know as well. This creates a greater likelihood that they'll be fully honest with themselves and those around them.

Talk About It

Once everyone who wishes to share has done so, use 5–10 minutes to conduct closure questions with the large group. Depending on the number of participants, you may need additional time to complete this part of the activity. Consider these discussion questions related to your group's experience:

- **What was it like to complete your "Becoming My Best" handout? What did you learn about the current choices in your life?**

- **Did you find it easy or difficult to complete the handout? Why? How did it feel to identify negative and positive influences in your life? Was it ever hard to be honest with yourself about who and what to write down?**

- **If there are people or things you need to change in your life, how will you go about doing that? How can others in this group help you make those changes?**

- **What did you learn that was new about others in the group? How can you use what people shared to strengthen this group?**

Wrapping Up

At the end of the meeting, teens may want to take their completed handouts home or place them in their notebooks or journals. You may also want to offer them the option of taking a blank handout with them so they can ask others who are important in their lives to complete the form. If they do this, encourage them to spend quiet time with that person or people talking about how they can help one another become their best.

Becoming My Best: Who Supports Me?

For each statement, think of the person or people who support you. Write their names in the corresponding sections of the form. You can write the same name in more than one section.

Love and Belonging
This person/these people:
- meet my need for love
- love me no matter what
- make me feel like I belong
- care about me and what happens to me
- are there in good times and bad

Achievement
This person/these people:
- respect my opinions
- make me feel important when I'm with them
- respect my skills and talents
- give me recognition and praise
- make me feel powerful

Love and Belonging | Achievement

Fun | Freedom

Fun
This person/these people:
- meet my need for fun
- share good times with me
- make me laugh when we're together
- enjoy having adventures when we're together
- are people I learn with when we're together

Freedom
This person/these people:
- meet my need for freedom
- allow me to be independent
- let me make my own decisions
- make me feel free to be myself
- allow me to make choices when we're together

From *Teambuilding with Teens: Activities for Leadership, Decision Making, and Group Success* by Mariam G. MacGregor, M.S., copyright © 2008. Free Spirit Publishing Inc., Minneapolis, MN; www.freespirit.com. This page may be photocopied for individual, classroom, and group work only. For all other uses, call 800-735-7323.

Becoming My Best: What Inspires Me?

For each statement, think of the activity or activities that support you in becoming your best. Write them in the corresponding sections of the form. You can write the same activity in more than one section.

Love and Belonging

When I do this activity/these activities, I feel like I belong to a team, family, club, or group.

Achievement

When I do this activity/these activities, I feel important and capable.

Love and Belonging | **Achievement**

Fun | **Freedom**

Fun

When I do this activity/these activities, I enjoy myself, make discoveries, and learn new things.

Freedom

When I do this activity/these activities, I feel in charge of myself, independent, able to make choices and decisions.

From *Teambuilding with Teens: Activities for Leadership, Decision Making, and Group Success* by Mariam G. MacGregor, M.S., copyright © 2008. Free Spirit Publishing Inc., Minneapolis, MN; www.freespirit.com. This page may be photocopied for individual, classroom, and group work only. For all other uses, call 800-735-7323.

Becoming My Best: Who Supports Me?

For each statement, think of the person or people who support you. Write their names in the corresponding sections of the form. You can write the same name in more than one section.

Love and Belonging

This person/these people:

- _____.
- _____.
- _____.
- _____.
- _____.

Achievement

This person/these people:

- _____.
- _____.
- _____.
- _____.
- _____.

Love and Belonging | Achievement

Fun | Freedom

Fun

This person/these people:

- _____.
- _____.
- _____.
- _____.
- _____.

Freedom

This person/these people:

- _____.
- _____.
- _____.
- _____.
- _____.

▶ MORE

From *Teambuilding with Teens: Activities for Leadership, Decision Making, and Group Success* by Mariam G. MacGregor, M.S., copyright © 2008. Free Spirit Publishing Inc., Minneapolis, MN; www.freespirit.com. This page may be photocopied for individual, classroom, and group work only. For all other uses, call 800-735-7323.

Becoming My Best: What Inspires Me?

For each statement, think of the activity or activities that support you in becoming your best. Write them in the corresponding sections of the form. You can write the same activity in more than one section.

Love and Belonging
When I do this activity/these activities, I

_____

_____

_____

_____

_____.

Achievement
When I do this activity/these activities, I

_____

_____

_____

_____

_____.

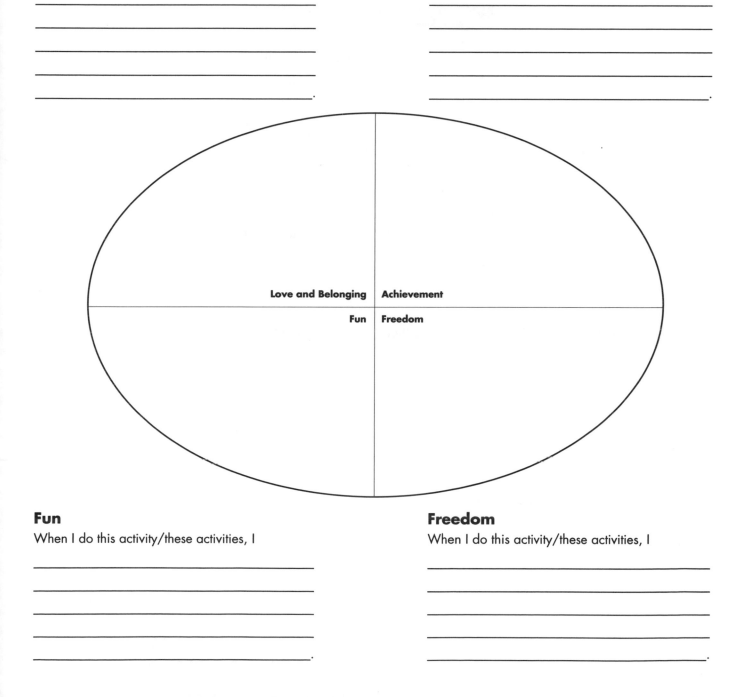

Love and Belonging | Achievement

Fun | Freedom

Fun
When I do this activity/these activities, I

_____

_____

_____

_____.

Freedom
When I do this activity/these activities, I

_____

_____

_____

_____.

From *Teambuilding with Teens: Activities for Leadership, Decision Making, and Group Success* by Mariam G. MacGregor, M.S., copyright © 2008. Free Spirit Publishing Inc., Minneapolis, MN; www.freespirit.com. This page may be photocopied for individual, classroom, and group work only. For all other uses, call 800-735-7323.

My Whole Self

LEARNING CONCEPTS

- Self-awareness • Personal values
- Balance and healthy life influences

(45 MINUTES)

This activity encourages teens to thoughtfully consider the different facets that make them a complete person. Since everyone will share a bit about who they are and how they see themselves, the activity also presents an opportunity for the group to determine how to become a "whole group," building on the varying perspectives of all members. Teens independently complete "My Whole Self" handouts and then share what they wrote with the group. A leadership-specific handout ("The Whole Leader") is included as a variation, as is the option to have participants create individual posters. The latter alternative allows you to refer to the posters for follow-up and can set the stage for group development activities related to balancing individual strengths and outlooks to build a stronger team.

GOALS

Participants will:
- learn how different facets of their personalities are connected
- learn more about how others see themselves
- identify similarities and differences in the group to determine ways to strengthen how the group works together

MATERIALS NEEDED

- Pen or pencil for each participant
- Handout: "My Whole Self" (page 33)
- *Optional*—Handout: "The Whole Leader" (page 34); newsprint, markers, and masking tape (see "Variations")

GETTING READY

Make copies of the "My Whole Self" handout for each teen.

If you are conducting this activity in a leadership-specific setting, make copies of "The Whole Leader" handout for each teen.

If you prefer to have participants create whole-self posters, use masking tape to hang sheets of newsprint (one for each teen) in different locations around the room. Have markers readily available. Draw a sample poster that has a larger version of the eight-section circle on the handout; label the sample "My Whole Self" or "The Whole Leader."

Setting the Stage

Having the basic knowledge that individuals are multi-dimensional is enough to guide you for setting the tone of this activity. The concept of whole-person education means helping individuals identify and develop the intellectual, spiritual, moral, and physical aspects of who they are. In essence, activities that emphasize the whole person are really about promoting wellness and balance in a person's outlook. Teens generally don't enjoy lectures about being well-rounded, yet by better understanding themselves, they may be able to learn more about working with others, managing stress, and developing healthy relationships. This activity is designed to nurture this understanding through self-discovery and group dialogue. It will have teens thinking about the unique perspectives they hold that make up who they are.

Throughout the activity, teens will explore the individual parts of themselves that contribute to them as complete people. There's value in pointing out to the group that people often notice only one characteristic about others, tending to focus on that single characteristic as a description of someone's full personality or as a means of labeling or categorizing the person. Drawing a math equation analogy of "the whole being greater than the sum of its parts," you can help teens see how their strengths and personalities come from combining many aspects of themselves. By helping teens see this in themselves, you can guide them to apply it to the others around them, stressing the importance of tapping into the "whole person" of every group member to create a stronger, more successful team.

Activity

Pass out a copy of the handout to each teen. Before they begin filling it out, explain the goal of the activity with words like these:

> **You all know that who you are is much more than what people see on the surface when they meet you. As you get to know others better and they get to know you, there are things about you that become more familiar. On this handout, finish each of the statements to describe yourself. Using single words, phrases, symbols, or drawings, write your responses to the sentence starters in each of the eight sections. You can write more than one description in each section. For example, for "I am" you might write about physical or cultural characteristics (such as "I am tall" or "I am Latina") or about relationships or interests (such as "I am a big brother" or "I am an athlete"). Take your time to reflect on each statement so you aren't just writing the most obvious things about yourself. You have 10 minutes to fill out the handout.**

After everyone is finished, bring the group together to share what they wrote and close the activity.

If you are focusing the activity on leadership, ask teens to complete each of the eight segments of "The Whole Leader" handout from the perspective of being a leader in your group or another. In the group discussion that follows, you may want to frame the questions with greater emphasis on leadership; however, the wording of the "Talk About It" questions is broad enough that they may work as they are with your group.

If you have prepared newsprint and a sample whole-self poster, have each teen choose a hanging sheet of newsprint and draw the same design you've put on the sample poster. Then teens can fill in the poster sections as described for the handouts. Prior to bringing participants together to discuss their posters, have the entire group walk around the poster "gallery" to see one another's posters. At each poster, ask the person who wrote it to describe it or answer any questions that others in the group may have.

Talk About It

Use 5–10 minutes at the end of the activity to help the group translate the individual nature of their handouts or posters to the group setting. You may want to consider these discussion questions:

- **What sections were the easiest and most difficult to complete? Why?**

- **How does this group recognize the different needs, hopes, beliefs, and other aspects of the members?**

- **After hearing or seeing what others wrote about themselves, how will you use this information to work better as a team?**

- **If there are certain strengths or perspectives missing from this group, how can you build those strengths or perspectives and promote everyone's skills in the group?**

- **How can you become "greater than the sum of your parts" as individual members and as an entire group?**

Wrapping Up

At the end of the session, and if space allows, hang all the handouts or posters around the room so others can view and read them when the group gathers again. If space doesn't allow, participants may take them home. Suggest that teens keep their completed handouts in their notebooks or journals for future reference.

My Whole Self

As a person . . .

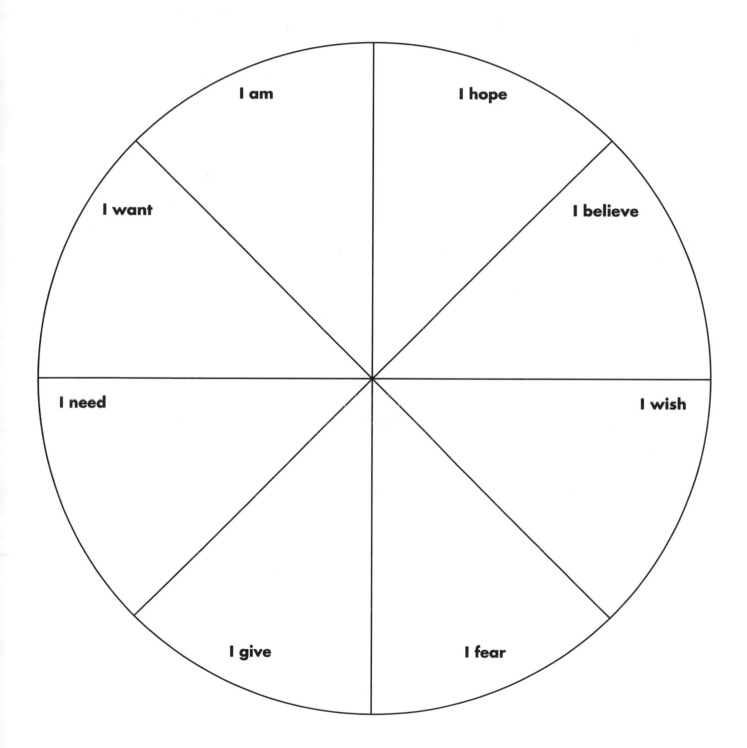

From *Teambuilding with Teens: Activities for Leadership, Decision Making, and Group Success* by Mariam G. MacGregor, M.S., copyright © 2008. Free Spirit Publishing Inc., Minneapolis, MN; www.freespirit.com. This page may be photocopied for individual, classroom, and group work only. For all other uses, call 800-735-7323.

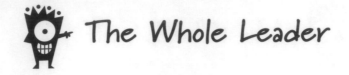 The Whole Leader

As a leader . . .

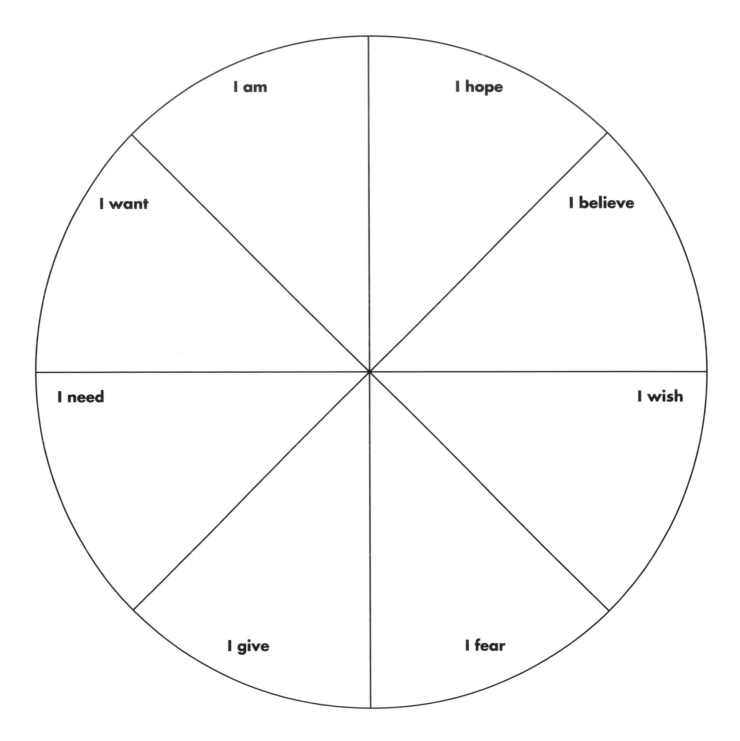

I am

I hope

I want

I believe

I need

I wish

I give

I fear

From *Teambuilding with Teens: Activities for Leadership, Decision Making, and Group Success* by Mariam G. MacGregor, M.S., copyright © 2008. Free Spirit Publishing Inc., Minneapolis, MN; www.freespirit.com. This page may be photocopied for individual, classroom, and group work only. For all other uses, call 800-735-7323.

Values Line

LEARNING CONCEPTS

- Self-awareness • Personal values
- Peer pressure, groupthink, and moral independence

(30–40 MINUTES)

Teens consider their personal values when asked to identify where they stand on an imaginary continuum between paired characteristics or concepts (such as Watcher/Doer, Journey/Destination, and so forth). Everyone will physically move to their spot on the continuum—based on what's important to them, what feels like the best fit, or what best represents them—and offer personal explanations as to why they chose that spot. You will need ample space for participants to move freely along a designated line in the room.

GOALS

Participants will:

- identify concepts and ideas that relate closely to who they are
- gain a basic understanding of personal values and standing up for one's beliefs
- learn more about others in the group and how they can work together in light of different values

MATERIALS NEEDED

- Masking tape
- Handout: "Sample Words for Values Line" (page 38)

GETTING READY

Make a copy of the "Sample Words for Values Line" handout for your own use. Depending on the space you are using to conduct this activity, move any tables, chairs, or desks out of the way to create an open area for movement. Tape a line of masking tape down the middle of the floor.

ACCOMMODATIONS

For groups where teens have physical challenges requiring crutches or a wheelchair, this activity can still be conducted as described; it may require a larger space for movement.

Setting the Stage

The handout provides a sample list of word pairs. Choose the pairs of words or phrases that work best for your group and time limit. You may want to add to or modify the list depending on the group's priorities and setting. In some cases, the paired words are (or can be) metaphors, such as *soccer/chess* or *tree/roots*, representing something beyond the actual words. Some of these words are followed by terms in parentheses to help you explain or define difficult concepts. With younger students, you may be inclined to use the simpler terms on the list; keep in mind that younger teens are extremely capable of thinking metaphorically because doing so calls on their imagination.

Prior to conducting the activity, you might want to introduce the topic of values and briefly explain that they are the things (individuals, beliefs, places, and so forth) that people find personally important and meaningful. Some values remain the same throughout life, while others change as a person grows older or gets involved in different activities or with different groups. Knowing your values is important; it allows you to make decisions more easily because you know exactly how you feel about something. Knowing what friends or families value also helps people stay true to their feelings and beliefs. This awareness allows individuals to maintain their own values while respecting the values of others. They can identify ideas everyone agrees upon and recognize where differences may arise.

The continuum used in this activity represents how people can share similar beliefs yet express them differently through their own personalities. For example, teens may become aware that they share a common view of themselves with others in their group, or they may relate to the same word but for different reasons. So in addition to illuminating the role values play, it's also helpful to spend time talking about how seeking out friends and teammates may mean looking beyond personalities to the underlying values or beliefs people hold.

Peer pressure can be an issue when using the continuum, and it is an important topic to address with this activity. You may want to talk about how *not* knowing one's values can create situations where others can put pressure on someone to do something the person may regret. It's also helpful to express one's values so others will know that certain lines can't (or won't) be crossed when working on a team project, arriving at decisions, or making social choices. (For another activity addressing peer pressure, see "Smirk," pages 19–22.)

The extension at the end of the activity highlights ways to further explore personal values or to have teens develop their own "values line" to use with peers or younger kids.

Activity

Ask teens to begin the activity by standing on either side of the masking tape line. Explain the activity by saying something like this:

> **In the middle of the room is a line that represents a *continuum*—a progression—of choices. I'm going to read some paired words or phrases. For each pair, one end of the continuum will represent the first word or phrase, and the other end will represent the second one. Listen to the words and decide which is more important to you—which word represents you better or feels like a better fit. Then decide where to stand along the line to show which idea you value and how much you value it. For example, if I say "forest/meadow," you'll decide whether to stand closer to the "forest" end of the continuum or the "meadow" end. You can stand anywhere on the line as long as you can explain why you are standing where you are. Some of the pairs of words are so distinctly different that you may find yourself easily picking one of the ends. With other pairs of words, you'll find it's harder to choose one end or the other. The middle of the line represents a choice of "It depends on the situation." Try not to stand in the middle; the goal here is for you to make a clear choice about where you fit on the line.**

After explaining the activity, slowly read each pair of words. Allow time for teens to move along the line with each pair you read. Take 1–2 minutes in each instance to have a few teens volunteer why they made the choice they did. Ask participants what the words mean to them, beyond the simplest definitions. This can be readdressed during the "Talk About It" discussion.

Once you have completed reading the list of words, ask teens to take a seat where they are.

Talk About It

Use about 10 minutes to talk about the activity. Even though questions about specific values aren't included here, you may want to spend time talking about whether this group or members of the group hold certain values and what those values are. Depending on what the group says, you can lead a discussion about how the group expresses those values and how it balances ideas and decisions when members believe different things are important. Consider these other discussion questions related to the activity:

- **What pairs of words on this list really made you think? Why?**

- **What other words do you think should have been on the list? Explain.**

- **Think about a time when most of you were at the same end. What about the few people at the other end? How can you prevent the group from ignoring or being insensitive to other people's views or ideas? How can you keep from seeming cliquish when most people—but not all—share the same beliefs or outlook?**

- **Are there situations where your friends or family expect you to act or believe a certain way even though you feel very differently? Did any of these feelings or thoughts occur for you during this activity? Explain.**

- **What situations in your life have tested your values the most? Did your personality, beliefs, or values change *during* the situation? Did your personality, beliefs, or values change *because* of the situation? Why or why not? If they did, in what ways did they change?**

- **Now that you know more about the different values and personalities that make up this group, will your views about how you can interact with others in the group change? Explain.**

Wrapping Up

Encourage teens to think and write about values in their notebooks or journals. Consider asking them to put together their own list of word pairs as part of their writing. If you wish, follow up this activity by using the extension idea for subsequent group meetings.

Extending the Learning

Do a teen-conducted activity with younger kids. Ask teens who are working with younger kids to create their own "values list" to use with the younger population. To get them started, have them think of concepts that younger kids relate to. For example, they can use different story, movie, or cartoon characters such as Tigger and Eeyore from "Winnie the Pooh." Using this pair, Tigger would represent energy, enthusiasm, and "going for it" while Eeyore would stand for being doubtful and extra careful.

Have them create a brief presentation or discussion about values, relating the topic to things kids find important in their lives right now; avoid having them look too far into the future. Once they have designed their list and brief discussion outline, have teens conduct the activity with a group of kids. After they've finished the workshop, guide a discussion with the teens in your group so they can reflect on what impact the experience had on their own values and beliefs.

Using what they learn from the workshop with younger kids, ask teens to think and write about the ways their values have changed over time. Also, have them interview someone much older than themselves about how the person's values have changed and what sorts of things influenced the changes.

Sample Words for Values Line

forest (protected)	meadow (exposed)
saver	spender
New York (city)	Montana (country)
captain	player
solitary	social (enjoys groups)
caretaker	taken care of
breakfast	dinner
talker	listener
teacher	student
watcher	doer
leader	follower
tortoise	hare
here (present)	there (future)
risk taker	cautious
director (vision)	actor (results)
soccer (physical)	chess (mental)
rainbow (journey)	pot of gold (destination)
straight line (rule follower)	curve (rule questioner)
mountain	valley
hybrid car	luxury car
thinker	feeler
spring	autumn
walking	running
read the book	watch the movie
organized	cluttered
unplanned	scheduled
unknown (accepts vagueness)	known (wants answers)
agree (positive/supportive)	disagree (negative/critical)
build (following plans or directions)	invent (flexible/creative)
facts	ideas
tree (end/outcome/seen)	roots (beginning/foundation/unseen)
justice (fairness)	mercy (compassion)
suit	jeans
Chihuahua	Labrador
tardy	punctual
peacemaker	judge

From *Teambuilding with Teens: Activities for Leadership, Decision Making, and Group Success* by Mariam G. MacGregor, M.S., copyright © 2008. Free Spirit Publishing Inc., Minneapolis, MN; www.freespirit.com. This page may be photocopied for individual, classroom, and group work only. For all other uses, call 800-735-7323.

Working with Others

Norms, Roles, and Expectations

House of Cards

Human Shuffle

The Mole

The Web

Norms, Roles, and Expectations

- Establishing group ground rules • Understanding others
- Teamwork and group dynamics

(45–60 MINUTES)

When individuals come together to form groups, it's important to talk about how each person works best and how the group can work together successfully. This activity allows teens to complete a series of open-ended statements on their own and then come together with others to discuss what each person expects to get from, and give to, the group. If the group is newly formed, this activity is a good icebreaker that helps set the tone for positive team dynamics. It's also a good activity to use if a group has been working together for some time and needs guidance on roles and behavior norms. If the group already has an identified leader, it's quite meaningful for this person to lead the sharing process, modeling norms and expectations while bringing the group together through discussion. Time permitting, you may want to allot two meeting periods.

GOALS

Participants will:

- identify how a new or existing team wants to work together
- learn how individual members view their role within the group
- learn how to set ground rules and clarify expectations in order to get the most from every member of the group
- be introduced to the concept of giving and receiving feedback

MATERIALS NEEDED

- Pen or pencil for each participant
- Markers
- 9 sheets of newsprint
- Masking tape
- Handout: "Norms, Roles, and Expectations" (pages 43–44)

40

GETTING READY

Make a copy of the "Norms, Roles, and Expectations" handout for each participant. On the newsprint, use a marker to write one of the nine statements from the handout on the top of each sheet. Tape the newsprint sheets around the room and have markers available.

Setting the Stage— What You Need to Know

For most organizations, *norms, roles,* and *expectations* are both spoken and unspoken. A delicate balance often exists between what is openly communicated and what people assume about being a member of the group. To set the tone for the activity, you will want to establish common definitions for these concepts and an understanding of why talking about them is important to group success. Consider these definitions to frame the activity and subsequent discussions.

Norm: A norm is a standard of behavior or a value that the group holds, which is understood to be typical or *normal* for the group (thus the word *norm*). Norms are determined by the group. Some norms are openly shared; others are unspoken, yet people understand them. Some shared group norms may include adhering to a meeting's scheduled starting time regardless of whether everyone is present or making it a practice to credit people for their contributions to the group.

Role: A member's role is the part the person takes in order to get things to happen. An obvious role is that of designated group leader; other roles may include promoters, information gatherers, or liaison agents with other clubs or groups. Sometimes the leader or the group assigns roles. At other times, an individual may volunteer for, or naturally take on, a role.

Expectation: This is something a member or members of the group expect to happen within the group or something members assume other members will think or do. For example, group members might have the expectation that others will be honest or will follow through and do what they say they'll do. Many times, expectations are left unspoken, so even though members may think others in a group hold the same expectations, they actually may not. For this reason, it's important for groups to discuss expectations.

The "Norms, Roles, and Expecations" handout includes a reference to receiving feedback. Some teens may be unfamiliar with what true feedback is, so it may be helpful to explain this term:

Feedback: Feedback refers to the comments group members offer to help each person become his or her best. Generally, feedback is given as a result of seeing or hearing something someone did. An example of effective feedback would be when one group member tells another member that she or he appreciated how the member took charge of a disorganized meeting. The most effective feedback is constructive and helps people make informed personal decisions and take action. It also is offered at an appropriate time and when a person is open to receiving it, not when tempers are high or a person is feeling defensive.

Activity

Pass out a "Norms, Roles, and Expectations" handout to each teen. Allow time for everyone to read through the statements. Then, prior to having teens complete the handout, take about 5 minutes to explain, define, and discuss the concepts and clarify the goals of the activity: to identify how the team wants to work together, understand how members perceive their roles, and determine what they expect from one another. As you discuss norms, roles, and expectations, make the terms real for teens by asking participants to apply them to the group. You might ask:

> **What is a norm (a role, an expectation)? What are examples of norms (roles, expectations) this group has?**

Remind participants to keep the meaning of the three terms in mind as they write their thoughts on the handout. Allow about 10 minutes for teens to complete the handouts. Let them know that they will be coming back together to talk about what they expect as part of this group. Say:

You'll share what you've written on the sheet, and once the group starts talking together about everyone's opinions, you'll want to feel that you've expressed yourself clearly. So, be honest with yourself. That way, you'll also be sure you've stated what you want others to know and haven't left something important unspoken. This helps set the stage for the group to work together successfully.

As teens are writing their responses, walk around the room to answer any questions or provide guidance if people get stuck on certain statements. One way to help move teens forward is to have them think of specific examples or behaviors they personally like or dislike in a group setting. Examples help teens keep things concrete, and when the group is having a discussion, they are able to say, "For example, when someone does this . . . it helps me think things through," or express similar ideas.

When all teens have completed their handouts, bring the group together to have everyone share what is written. Ask for one or more volunteers to summarize ideas on the newsprint sheets. If the group has an existing leader, ask him or her to lead the discussion, providing assistance or prompts as needed to help when someone's answers are unclear. As you summarize, you will also be able to keep the group on task so everyone is able to share their opinions, especially if certain comments really resonate with the group and lead participants on a tangent.

The discussion at this point should feel open and honest, with individuals readily acknowledging what others are saying and asking additional questions, if needed, to clarify what's being said. As with brainstorming, you'll want to remind people that the goal isn't to criticize or put down what others say. Rather it's to establish, both verbally and visually (using the newsprint), the norms, roles, and expectations that individual members have as they relate to successfully working together as a group.

Allow 30–35 minutes or more for everyone to share and discuss their comments before going on to the "Talk About It" discussion.

Talk About It

Use 5–10 minutes to bring the activity to a close and to help the group identify any necessary next steps to put what they've learned into action. Consider these discussion questions:

- **What new things did you learn about everyone's view of this group? After doing this activity, what beliefs of your own are clearer? Which have changed? Which do you look at differently now?**

- **How can you use the information from this activity to improve the way this group works together in the future?**

- **How can you best use the strengths and talents of group members while also allowing everyone a chance to try new things or use new talents when working together?**

- **Based on this activity, if the group were to assign "official" roles for each member, what roles do you think people should have?** (Offer an example such as, "For instance, Karla shared a lot about being creative, so maybe she could be the lead publicity person.")

- **Would you want to do this activity again after the group has worked together for a while? Why or why not?**

Wrapping Up

If space allows, keep the newsprint hanging in the room for future meetings. If space doesn't allow, you may want to type or have a volunteer type the information from the summary sheets and pass them out for teens to keep in their notebooks or journals.

Norms, Roles, and Expectations

1. I want my role in this group to be:

_____

_____

_____

2. Something that is important to know about me when I'm part of a group is:

_____

_____

_____

3. I expect to get the following from others in our group:

_____

_____

_____

4. Others in this group can expect to get this from me:

_____

_____

5. I expect all members of the group to:

_____

_____

_____

From *Teambuilding with Teens: Activities for Leadership, Decision Making, and Group Success* by Mariam G. MacGregor, M.S., copyright © 2008. Free Spirit Publishing Inc., Minneapolis, MN; www.freespirit.com. This page may be photocopied for individual, classroom, and group work only. For all other uses, call 800-735-7323.

6. I hope our group holds these norms:

_____

_____

_____

7. When others give me feedback, whether positive or negative, I appreciate:

_____

_____

_____

8. As a group member, I get frustrated when these things don't happen within a group:

_____

_____

_____

9. As a member of this group, I'm still unsure about:

_____

_____

_____

From *Teambuilding with Teens: Activities for Leadership, Decision Making, and Group Success* by Mariam G. MacGregor, M.S., copyright © 2008. Free Spirit Publishing Inc., Minneapolis, MN; www.freespirit.com. This page may be photocopied for individual, classroom, and group work only. For all other uses, call 800-735-7323.

House of Cards

(45 MINUTES)

The object of this activity is to allow the group to focus on how they make decisions to accomplish a goal. It promotes teamwork, the development of communication skills, and discussions on group dynamics. Throughout the activity, teens remain silent except during designated discussion times, and so group members must figure out how to use resources and set goals using only nonverbal communication. The larger group is divided into two or more small groups who complete the first part of the activity as separate, competing teams. After a brief discussion period, the small groups are asked to join together to accomplish a larger goal that requires teamwork instead of competition. You will need ample floor or tabletop space for all teams to work on creating three-dimensional houses of cards, with room for individual houses to be connected to one another.

GOALS

Participants will:

- work as a team using limited resources and no verbal communication
- clarify challenges that can arise even with an obvious group goal in mind
- strengthen nonverbal communication skills

MATERIALS NEEDED

- Large supply (1,000 or more) of 3" x 5" index cards, library cards, or playing cards (about 20 decks)

GETTING READY

Depending on the space you use to conduct this activity, move any tables, chairs, or desks out of the way or together to create an open area for movement and building. Also, be prepared with a method of dividing your larger group into smaller teams without allowing participants to select their own teammates. Have the cards in a central location where all teams will have easy access while building. The more teams you have, the more cards you will need.

ACCOMMODATIONS

For groups where teens have physical challenges requiring crutches or a wheelchair, this activity can still be conducted as described. It may be necessary for teams to work on desks or tabletops instead of on the floor. Move tables or desks as close to one another as possible, since the second part of the activity asks teams to connect their individual houses together. For teens with limited manual dexterity, this activity will be challenging; they may require assistance handling the cards to design and set up the houses.

Setting the Stage

There are two parts to this activity. During Part 1, each team works independently to build a house of cards. During Part 2, the teams work together to connect the houses. Both times, teens must complete the tasks using only nonverbal communication. Speaking will take place during the designated "Talk About It" discussions.

Activity: Part 1

Divide the entire group into two or more smaller teams, each with five to eight members. Do not allow teens to select their team members; count off or use some other neutral mechanism for creating the teams. Once the teams have been identified, assign each team its own spot in the room, with teams in reasonable proximity of one another in order to facilitate the second part of the activity.

Explain the activity like this:

Each of your teams will create a three-dimensional house of cards from the ground up. You will have 15 minutes to create your houses, using only the cards. You may not use table legs, chairs, books, tape, paper clips, or any other items to support your houses. There are two other rules: First, you cannot communicate verbally with each other to accomplish your goal—this means no talking, grunting, humming, or other mouth sounds. Second, you cannot draw or illustrate any of your ideas. You have only the set time to finish the house; if it falls at any time during those 15 minutes, start over. Giving up isn't an option. You want everyone in your group to be satisfied with the final structure.

Mention other instructions if you wish, such as that no cards can be bent or torn. Be sure to mention this at the beginning because groups can get ultra-creative about how they build! Take care not to set up the activity as a competition between teams; this tends to naturally occur and can be a point for discussion. As teams start building, watch to make sure groups keep their houses freestanding, with no support from other objects or items. Let them know when they have 5 minutes left.

After time has been called, have the groups move away from the structures (and perhaps into a larger group circle) so that you can discuss Part 1 of the activity.

Talk About It: Part 1

Take about 5 minutes to discuss questions such as these that address working on the individual houses in the small groups:

- **What was it like to have to work in silence with your team to accomplish your goal? What techniques did you rely on to communicate?**

- **How did you know when everyone in your group was satisfied and had achieved its goal?**

- **How did your group deal with frustration? For example, if your house fell down at all, how did your group react and get going again?**

- **Did you feel like you were competing against the other groups? Why or why not?**

Activity: Part 2

After discussing the first part of the activity, inform the separate teams that they will now work as a full team and connect all of the structures together using more cards. The rules of nonverbal communication with no writing or drawing still apply. The connecting structure must also be three-dimensional, with no other support systems. Again, the connection is not complete until everyone in the group is satisfied. Allow 10–15 minutes for teams to work together to accomplish this.

Talk About It: Part 2

Use the final 5–10 minutes to talk about both Part 2 and the activity overall. Consider these discussion questions related to your group's experience:

- **This time, what was it like to be told the goal and to have to work with the entire group to accomplish it?**

- **How did your group know when everyone was satisfied and had achieved its goal?**

- **Did anyone emerge as a leader? Who and why?**

- **How did the attitude of competition change when working on the goal this time?**

- **How would this activity have been different if you could have communicated verbally?**

Wrapping Up

Consider challenging teens to observe how people (themselves included) use nonverbal skills and rely on other strategies for communicating with others. If you ask them to to do this, take 5–10 minutes at the next meeting to have them share what they observed. If time doesn't allow for this discussion, or if your group won't meet again for some time, encourage teens to write in their notebooks or journals about their experience of nonverbal communication and teamwork throughout the activity.

Human Shuffle

- Teamwork and group dynamics • Communication skills
- Setting and achieving a goal

(35–45 MINUTES)

In this activity, the group forms a single-file line along an established narrow path constructed from boards or demarcated with tape. Although the entire group is working toward a common goal, you will separate them in the middle, so there are two "teams" standing on the path facing each other, like strings of cars meeting on a single-lane road. The goal is for each team member to move from his or her position to the "mirror" position on the opposite end of the line without stepping off the path. This is not a competition; participants are challenged to strategize and cooperate as a team across the entire line. You will need ample space lengthwise to lay out the planks or tape and allow for safe movement.

GOALS

Participants will:

- learn to work as a team
- strengthen communication skills
- clarify challenges that can arise even with an obvious group goal in mind

MATERIALS NEEDED

- 1" x 6" x 8' wood planks, one plank for every 5–6 participants (available at hardware and home improvement stores; planks not exceeding 8' fit into an average-sized car if you need to transport them)

or

- Masking or duct tape (2–3" wide) that can be removed easily from the floor after use

GETTING READY

Depending on the space you use to conduct this activity, move any tables, chairs, or desks out of the way to create a long, open area for movement. On the floor, place the planks end to end to create a narrow path approximately 20–30 feet long, depending on the number of participants. The path will carry two subgroups of eight or fewer members each; if your entire group is larger than 16, you will want to have two separate structured paths. This allows everyone to get involved, avoid falling off, and accomplish the goal within the time frame.

If using the tape, lay it on the floor to a length of 20–30 feet. Place at least three or four strips of tape next to each other for the entire length, creating a walking path that is 8–9 inches wide.

In most situations, using the wood planks is recommended because they physically lift teens off the ground. This slight lift encourages them to pay closer attention to staying on the path and decreases the likelihood that they'll try to accomplish the goal without really staying within the rules of the game.

ACCOMMODATIONS

For groups where teens have physical challenges requiring crutches or a wheelchair, this activity is challenging, but it can be done. The members of the group will need to work together to set ground rules for accommodating any teens with challenges without compromising the overall goal of the activity. In this case it is recommended to create the path using tape in order to avoid having to deal with the lift created by wood planks.

Activity

Before introducing the activity, have participants line up single file on the planks or tape. Based on the number of teens in the group, divide them into two equal subgroups and indicate where the middle space is between them. Then explain the activity:

You're going to do an activity called the "Human Shuffle." This is not a competition. The object of this activity is for everyone on one side of the line to exchange places with everyone on the other side *without stepping off the path*. You're divided into two "teams" based on where the middle of the line is, but really you all need to work together to achieve the goal. You can keep moving forward, but you cannot move backward, and you will ultimately change places exactly; for example, if you are third in line now, you'll be third in line when you have moved to the other side of the path. By exchanging places, you will create a mirror reflection of what your group looks like now. So take a minute to see who is in the same spot as you on the other part of the line.

Allow a minute or two to let students step off the line to see who they'll be switching places with. Then continue:

Imagine that all around the path is a cold, rushing river. Anyone who steps off the path will be pulled downstream through the whitewater and need to be rescued. This means that if a person steps off, even with just one foot, the entire group must start over again. (If a group has worked together for

some time, you may want to add more challenge. For example, you could add a rule that if a person steps off the line, the group not only has to begin again, but that person loses the use of the leg that touched the imaginary water.) **You have 25 minutes to accomplish your goal. Use that time to strategize, try out plans, and get everyone moved forward. Before you start strategizing or moving, I'll answer any questions you have. Then I'll start keeping time.**

Take 3–5 minutes to answer any questions. If the group starts strategizing or moving, inform them that time has started.

There is no single way to accomplish this goal. Participants can pass people over, under, or around them; they may find that leapfrog moves seem to work for their group. As the teens start moving people around, you'll want to emphasize safety. If necessary, ask them to refrain from certain methods, such as lifting people too high. If the group does not complete the task in 25 minutes, allow them to negotiate for additional time in 2-minute increments, encouraging them to use the least amount of extra time needed.

When the group has accomplished the goal, congratulate them and encourage them to acknowledge their success before bringing everyone together to talk about their experience and apply what they learned.

Talk About It

Take 10 minutes to talk about the activity. Consider these discussion questions related to your group's experience:

- Once you knew what you needed to do, how did you decide how you were going to accomplish the goal? Do you feel you spent too much or not enough time strategizing? Explain.

- Did someone emerge as a leader? If so, how did this work for your group? If not, how would things have gone for the group if one person did all the directing and the others followed?

- How did people introduce new ideas and make suggestions? How did it feel when others did or didn't listen to your ideas?

- What did you learn about how your group communicates with one another? About how you make decisions?

- When people stepped off the line and you had to start again, how did the group react? What does this tell you about how this group works together?

Wrapping Up

Suggest that teens identify everyday situations where both strategizing and trial and error are necessary to succeed. In addition to writing in their journals or notebooks about the experience of working as a team to achieve this goal, ask them to write about real-life situations that reinforce this activity.

The Mole

LEARNING CONCEPTS

- Teamwork and group dynamics
- Trust and distrust • Problem solving

(35–45 MINUTES)

This activity demonstrates how dynamics change when distrust arises in a group. The group attempts to solve a problem without the guidance of a leader. At the beginning of the process, suspicion is raised when you tell participants that there may be a "mole" in the group trying to prevent the team from succeeding. In actuality there is not a mole, but the dynamics of the group make everyone believe otherwise.

In a partitioned area of the room you will set up a three-dimensional structure made of playing cards. In another part of the room, teams of students work to build an exact replica of the model, relying on fellow group members to make sure they are building the structure correctly. As they work, they begin to suspect their own teammates of providing inaccurate clues for building it. Some groups might not finish the task because of suspicious attitudes, and some participants may find it difficult to confront others for seemingly not trying to help the team. Regardless of whether groups complete the task, the activity and discussion bring up issues of trust and group dynamics that apply beyond this group setting to everyday life.

You will need a room with a small partitioned area where the original design can be set up and obscured from view and additional space so groups of teens can move around freely. Each team needs a desk or table to work on.

GOALS

Participants will:

- learn to confront issues of distrust
- strengthen their understanding of how attitudes (positive and negative) affect group dynamics
- clarify how to solve problems and achieve goals despite possible roadblocks

MATERIALS NEEDED

- Decks of playing cards (one deck for every 6–8 participants plus one for the model structure)
- Standard-size (approximately 3½" x 6") envelopes (one for each participant)
- Pen
- Stapler

- Handouts: "Team Instructions for Building a Card Structure Replica" and "Special Mole Instructions" (page 55)

GETTING READY

Copy enough "Team Instructions for Building a Card Structure Replica" and "Special Mole Instructions" handouts for each participant. On each copy of the "Special Mole Instructions," mark *by hand* an X on the line next to "You ARE NOT the mole." It is important that you mark the same thing on every sheet, to establish that there isn't a mole in the group. Place each sheet in an envelope, seal all the envelopes, and staple one envelope behind each copy of the "Team Instructions for Building a Card Structure Replica."

Prior to conducting the activity, use one deck of cards to construct an original card structure in the partitioned area of the room. This will be the model for the replica structures the teams will build; make it three-dimensional and use as many cards as possible. Make sure the model is not visible to teens as they enter the room or as you explain the activity.

Determine how you will divide your larger group into smaller groups of six to eight members.

Setting the Stage

Most people don't join a group or team thinking that others in the group will have different goals than they do. Typically, people want to start off with a positive attitude and an assumption that everyone's agenda is the same, that all are dedicated to achieving the group's objectives.

Believing others have an underlying agenda or ulterior motive creates distrust and suspicion in groups that may otherwise be successful. Members begin to question others and challenge group decisions, often resulting in a general breakdown of how the group works together. In this activity, the effect may not be so dramatic. The atmosphere that arises, however, provides a starting point to openly discuss ways to establish group expectations, improve deteriorating team relationships, or confront existing dynamics where someone has or seems to have undermined the group's goals.

Groups of younger teens are likely to approach the activity with a more direct approach. They may more openly blame or accuse others, even jokingly, due to a tendency to speak the truth sooner. Older teens may try to figure out who is attempting to sabotage the group and may be more subtle, or even subversive, when trying to confront other members. If there is an existing outspoken member or someone who is often a scapegoat, group members may believe from the get-go that this person is to blame—a situation that provides an uncomfortable yet effective opportunity to challenge the group to change its existing interactions or judgments of each other.

In the unlikely event that teens become sarcastic or mean-spirited toward certain members, it may be necessary to step in and remind them to focus on the activity and not to bring up personal things from the past. If comments become deliberately cutting, or if you view ostracizing behavior that isn't related to the activity, take a minute or two to refocus the group on the real goal of the exercise. Openly point out the behavior that is occurring and challenge teens to participate purposefully in the activity. "Extending the Learning" at the end of this activity allows you to further explore ways to improve trust and constructively confront group members.

Activity

When teens arrive, divide them into smaller groups of six to eight people. Ask each team to select a desk or table. Place a deck of cards in the center of each group's work surface without designating a leader in any of the groups; do not ask the teams to choose a leader. Then say:

On your table is a deck of cards that your team will need to complete a task. I am passing out instruction sheets and secret envelopes to everyone in your group. You may read through the instruction sheet, but do *not* open the envelope attached to it until I tell you to.

Pass out the instruction sheets with the envelope stapled to them and go over the "Team Instructions for Building a Card Structure Replica" together, letting teens know the location of the concealed area. Then continue:

When you open your envelope, you will find "Special Mole Instructions." Keep the information on these special instructions a secret until after your group has finished building the replica house of cards. Put the special instruction sheet back in the envelope or in your pocket—just make sure no one else sees what's in your envelope. This is not a competition among teams; you're to work as hard as you can within your individual team to accomplish the goal. Let me know when you want me to check out your project. I'll tell you if there are mistakes, but I won't say specifically what is wrong. You have 15 minutes to complete the task. Open your envelopes.

Once teens have opened their envelopes and the groups have begun working, walk around the room monitoring and observing what happens. If necessary, jot notes to keep track of things you want to bring up when the groups are done. As teams ask you to check out their structures, do so without drawing attention from the other groups. If there are mistakes, avoid being specific about what they are. Allow the group to keep working together in an attempt to fix their replica. Let groups know when 5 minutes remain. Regardless of whether the groups accurately complete the replicas, end the process when 15 minutes have elapsed. After calling time, remove the partition shielding the model. Give groups a few minutes to look at the model structure, compare it to theirs, and decompress a little in their small groups before bringing everyone together to talk about what happened.

Talk About It

Use about 15 minutes to talk about the activity. Begin by asking:

Who was the mole in each group?

When no one speaks up, allow participants to react. Then say:

No one? Then what happened in this activity?

Provide time for each group to explain their experiences and for you to offer any of your own observations that stood out. Allow flexibility for discussion time, as some touchy issues may come up during the process. Some teens might, for example, be upset about how people treated others in their group, about actions that could be perceived as cheating, or about comments referring to outside behaviors that were made in the context of the activity ("That's just like Joe. I could see him being the mole, he never supports our group's goals"). Openly point out the comments or flashpoints as you observe them, and allow the group to process them during this discussion time.

Also discuss some or all of the following questions related to your group's experience:

- Maybe others in your group accused you of being the mole, or maybe you suspected someone of being the mole. If so, what went on in your mind? What behaviors made each of you suspicious that someone was a mole? Did you ever want to just come out and ask others if they were the mole? *Did* you ask? Why? What happened?

- How did the way your group worked together change as the activity went along? What would you do in a real-life group situation if you thought a team member was working against you or others in the group? If your group didn't complete the replica, what would need to have happened so you could have done so?

- Sometimes trust is broken in a group. This can happen whether it's a group of friends, your family, a sports team, a counseling group, or another one. When this happens, how can people reestablish trust?

- What steps can a group take to make sure everyone is working for the same goal? When people start going in different directions, what can you do to keep the group productive?

Wrapping Up

Because this activity deals with trusting others, ask teens to spend some time over the next few days evaluating the role trust plays in their lives. Suggest they watch how they interact with friends and family members, what it takes for them to trust others, and how they can tell when someone is distrustful. You may also ask them to bring in newspaper or magazine clippings on how public figures gain and lose the trust of their supporters and critics. Encourage teens to write their observations and opinions about trust, distrust, confronting problems, and establishing or reestablishing a solid group connection in their notebooks or journals.

Extending the Learning

This activity has multiple levels of learning. In particular, you may want to focus the group on two different, yet related, topics: improving trust and identifying ways to confront others who may not be working toward mutual goals.

Participate in a ropes course. To address trust issues, consider having teens participate in low-elements activities at a ropes course if you have one in your area. These activities can be facilitated by the ropes course staff after you provide them with information about the issues you want the group to work through. To locate a ropes course facility near you, contact one of the following:

Association for Challenge Course Technology (www.acctinfo.org)

Professional Ropes Course Association (www.prcainfo.org)

Project Adventure (www.pa.org)

You can also look in the Yellow Pages in your area under "Ropes Courses," "Challenge Courses," or "Conference Centers."

Watch and discuss _The Abilene Paradox_. To further explore the issue of productively confronting others in a group, consider showing the video _The Abilene Paradox_, available at most libraries. You can also rent the video from ATS Media (www.atsmedia.com). The movie doesn't address having a mole in a group; rather, it explores how groups make decisions based on the belief that everyone shares the same opinion. It also highlights how problems in a group can escalate when people wait too long to voice their true opinions.

Team Instructions for Building a Card Structure Replica

In the area of the room that you can't see is a three-dimensional model made of playing cards. Your team's task is to construct a *replica*—a structure that is identical to the model—in the shortest amount of time. You have up to 15 minutes to complete the task. The replica must be correct. The shape must be the same as the model and all cards need to be in the correct position.

Any team member can go to view the original design. However, this must be done *one person at a time only.* That person may look at the original as long as she or he wishes. People may go back and look again as often as your group decides is necessary.

When you believe your replica is correct, notify me and I will check your structure. If it's incorrect, I'll tell you there is at least one mistake, although I won't tell you what or where it is. You'll continue working on the structure.

From *Teambuilding with Teens: Activities for Leadership, Decision Making, and Group Success* by Mariam G. MacGregor, M.S., copyright © 2008. Free Spirit Publishing Inc., Minneapolis, MN; www.freespirit.com. This page may be photocopied for individual, classroom, and group work only. For all other uses, call 800-735-7323.

- -

Special Mole Instructions (FOR YOUR EYES ONLY)

Perhaps you've heard of a "mole." In the world of espionage, a mole is a double agent, secretly working against a group he or she is part of. In real-life situations, all team members don't always work toward the same goals. Sometimes people do things to reach personal objectives rather than team goals. They may also work against team goals because of group tension, lack of trust, difficulty getting along with others, or other reasons.

There may be such a person in your group today. You can think of that person as "The Mole." It's also possible that there's more than one mole in the group.

If you are the mole, you're to do everything in your power to work against the efforts of your group, *without letting anyone know you're the mole.*

If a team member thinks another team member is the mole, he or she can accuse that person. The rest of the group will vote, and if there's unanimous agreement, the group can exclude the mole from any further planning or discussion with the group.

_____ You ARE the mole.

_____ You ARE NOT the mole.

From *Teambuilding with Teens: Activities for Leadership, Decision Making, and Group Success* by Mariam G. MacGregor, M.S., copyright © 2008. Free Spirit Publishing Inc., Minneapolis, MN; www.freespirit.com. This page may be photocopied for individual, classroom, and group work only. For all other uses, call 800-735-7323.

The Web

- Teamwork and group dynamics • Communication skills
- Problem solving and working through crisis

(30–45 MINUTES)

Many groups run into tough times, especially when people forget how they fit into their group, how others rely on them, or what their role is. This activity can solidify the group's understanding that everyone can contribute. It's useful when a group is struggling or a few members feel like they're carrying the weight of the team. Teens are organized into a circle and given a long piece of string that winds from person to person to create a symbolic web. As you read a

series of statements, team members are asked to step out one by one, dropping their piece of the web and leaving the others to pick up the slack created by their departure. As fewer teens are left in the group, keeping the web intact becomes difficult and the remaining teens find themselves moving farther away from one another. Both the process and the final result provide plenty to talk about after the experience. You will need a reasonably large space or room for movement.

GOALS

Participants will:

- understand what's needed to keep a group going
- learn to work as a team in spite of other pressures
- identify areas where the group needs to solve problems or communicate better

MATERIALS NEEDED

- Scissors
- Roll of string or yarn (ample amount)

- Handouts: "Web Key Words" (pages 59–60) and "Web Statements" (pages 61–62)

GETTING READY

Make one copy of the "Web Key Words." If you would like to use additional or different words with your group, write the words and their definitions in the spaces provided. Cut the words and explanations into individual slips and fold them in half once to hide the information on each word slip.

Review the activity directions. Then copy and read through the "Web Statements"; write in any words you have added along with corresponding statements. The statements finish with the words *leadership* and *vision;* consider which two words you want to finish with and organize the statements to reflect this.

If using an indoor room, create a large open space by pushing chairs and desks to the edge of the room.

Setting the Stage

Most groups have a tendency to rely on the same people for every job or have members who are routinely the first to volunteer. Every group faces difficult times as well. When emotions flare, group members may begin to forget what their purpose is, both as individuals and as team players. Taking time before a group is embroiled in a crisis to reevaluate and reconnect can pay off by opening the lines of communication. Even if a group is in the middle of a struggle, it can be helpful to spend time doing an activity that focuses energy back on the job everyone is supposed to be doing.

Although this activity is carefully structured, the symbolism it evokes may lead to emotionally charged conversations. If necessary, allocate time for people to honestly speak their minds. Teens may bring up factors that are affecting how the group is working together. You'll want to be able to address this and provide a safe venue for individuals in the group to respond to and talk about how others are feeling. Make sure to maintain positive group norms and ground rules for a productive conversation so it doesn't turn into an "us and them" sort of atmosphere. And be certain to close the discussion in a manner that allows the group to move forward and let go of anything hindering their success. (See "Setting the Tone," pages 3–6, for more on setting a positive group environment.)

Activity

Ask teens to form a tight circle in the middle of the room. If you have more teens than you have word slips, identify the teens who will serve as observers to the exercise (like watching a fishbowl). Ask observers to keep quiet and watch what happens in the circle. If the number of participants allows the entire group to be involved in the circle, mention to teens that there will come a time in the activity when they will become observers. Explain the activity like this:

> I'm going to pass out a slip of paper to each of you. On the paper is a word and definition. Don't reveal what your slip says until I ask you to. I'm also going to give you a roll of string that you'll use to create a web that connects you with each other. To do this, the person I give the loose end to will toss the roll of string across the circle to another person. The next person will do the same, tossing it across to another person. You can pass the string to whomever you like *except* the person standing right beside you. Everyone should be holding part of the string, and the string *should not touch the ground.* The final person to receive the roll of string will hold onto it for the activity. This person cannot wind the string up at all at any time. Please don't let go of your portion of the string.

Pass out the slips before giving teens the roll of string. Give the word slips with the final two words (*leadership* and *vision,* or two words you have determined) to teens on opposite sides of the circle from one another; these two people cannot be next to each other. Do not indicate to these students or to the group that their words are in any way significant.

Hand the loose end of the roll of string to a teen who holds one of the final two words. Starting with this person, guide the group as they toss the roll of string across the circle to each member of the group until everyone is holding onto a section of the string. Visually, this will create a symbolic spider's web parallel to the ground. Continue explaining the activity by saying:

> Imagine that you're all connected to one another like part of a large spider web. Your goal is to keep your web taut and off the ground as long as you can. So hang on and, one by one, please read your word and its definition from your slips of paper.

In no particular order, ask teens to read the words and definitions on their slips before you begin to read your statements. To introduce your statements, say:

Thank you. Now I'm going to read you statements about your words and how they fit together. As I read your word, you are to step *out* of the circle and release your portion of the web. The remaining people will have to pick up the slack in order to keep all of the web off the ground. No matter how many or how few of you remain holding the web, you're to keep it up from the ground and as tight as possible for as long as you can. Let's begin.

Read the "Web Statements" aloud. Take your time between words so teens can move themselves and still keep the string up. As teens step out, indicate where you want them to stand so they can observe what takes place; remind them to remain quiet until the end. When you've finished the statements and the last two teens are left standing (probably very far from one another and really struggling to keep the string off the ground), invite everyone back together to talk about the experience and apply what they've learned.

Talk About It

Allow the room to remain silent for a few minutes as people think about the activity. This can raise powerful responses and thoughts, especially if the group is facing or has recently dealt with a difficult period in their work together. When people have had a few minutes for contemplation, ask questions about the activity such as these:

- **What stands out most from this activity?** If you had observers, ask: **Observers, what did you observe? What feedback do you have for the group? What did you learn that relates to the group in general?**

- As time went on, how did it feel to have to leave the circle? What was it like to be left in the circle?

- How does this activity reinforce the positive and negative things happening in this group on an everyday basis?

- In what ways does this group communicate about each person's role in it? Who does the group rely on to get things done? How do you talk about things if you feel people aren't doing their part?

- Was there a point where you felt it would be impossible to keep the web together? If so, when? If not, what made you confident you could keep it together?

- Does this group need to change how things are being done in order to be more successful or better prepared for challenging situations or crisis? If in real life the group were falling apart as this web activity symbolized, what would need to happen to bring your group back together? Share some ideas.

Wrapping Up

Building on the web analogy, ask teens to think about other groups they belong to and the ways the members are connected like a web. Suggest that they observe key people in one of the groups and think about what would happen to the group if those people were no longer members. Encourage them to write their thoughts in their journals or notebooks, or if they can, to arrange a time for that group to talk about the issues raised in this activity, including how the group can address disproportionate member contributions.

Web Key Words

Friendship: A positive, supportive relationship with others

Support: Upholding, believing in, and helping others or your cause

Trust: Confidence and belief in someone or something

Cooperation: Willingness to work with others

Recognition: Noticing and appreciating others

Organization: Putting things together in an orderly way

Adaptability: Ability to change or be flexible for different situations

Fairness: Treating others alike

Decision Making: Choosing among options to reach a solution

Respect: Treating others with honor and courtesy

Understanding: Knowing or being able to relate to how others feel

Motivation: Being inspired to get things done

Creativity: Ability to think in new and original ways

From *Teambuilding with Teens: Activities for Leadership, Decision Making, and Group Success* by Mariam G. MacGregor, M.S., copyright © 2008. Free Spirit Publishing Inc., Minneapolis, MN; www.freespirit.com. This page may be photocopied for individual, classroom, and group work only. For all other uses, call 800-735-7323.

Communication: Expressing thoughts, feelings, and information to and with others

Empathy: Ability to put yourself in someone else's place and understand how the person feels

Approachability: Making others feel that they can talk or work with you easily

Dependability: Being trustworthy and reliable

Risk Taking: Taking a chance without knowing if you'll succeed or fail

Vision: Ability to imagine what can happen in the future

Leadership: Ability to guide the way

From *Teambuilding with Teens: Activities for Leadership, Decision Making, and Group Success* by Mariam G. MacGregor, M.S., copyright © 2008. Free Spirit Publishing Inc., Minneapolis, MN; www.freespirit.com. This page may be photocopied for individual, classroom, and group work only. For all other uses, call 800-735-7323.

Web Statements

Before the activity, add your own additional words and statements to this form if you wish. During the activity, read the words and statements one by one. As you complete each statement, have the individual holding that word step out of the string web. Remind the rest of the group to pick up the slack left by team members' departure.

Friendship: Lately it seems that people just haven't been getting along. You need to step to the side and try to figure out why.

Support: Since people aren't as friendly with each other, you've had to work extra hard. You're getting tired, so take a rest.

Trust: People are starting to question each other and have little faith in the rest of the team. You aren't sure how to change things. Why not take a seat and try to find some answers.

Cooperation: People are having more and more problems working together. No one wants to help. Maybe you need to stop and figure out a new approach.

Recognition: With all the unhappiness, you can't seem to give enough praise and recognition to keep everyone happy. Do you need a new reward system? Step out and think it over.

Organization: With fewer helpers, everything is getting harder to do. Everyone is busy trying to survive, and you just can't keep it all together. You're giving up and getting out.

Adaptability: You've been busy helping everybody deal with the changes in the group, but enough is enough! Take a break.

Fairness: You are so busy trying to keep everyone happy that you are starting to get too involved and can't stay objective. Get out of there!

Decision Making: There are simply too few members who care about coming to a decision. You are getting very confused and need some help, so you've decided it's time to remove yourself from the scene.

Respect: What respect? Everyone seems caught up in their own world, people are snapping or yelling at each other, and you feel useless. Why not go sit on the sidelines?

Understanding: You've had it! You're tired of working hard to stay on top of everyone's needs and keep everything going smoothly. Right now it feels like a tidal wave is ready to crash. Get out while you can.

Motivation: Morale is horrible, and you can't have everyone relying on you, because you're burned out. Give it up.

From *Teambuilding with Teens: Activities for Leadership, Decision Making, and Group Success* by Mariam G. MacGregor, M.S., copyright © 2008. Free Spirit Publishing Inc., Minneapolis, MN; www.freespirit.com. This page may be photocopied for individual, classroom, and group work only. For all other uses, call 800-735-7323.

Creativity: You've run out of new approaches and aren't feeling very creative. You need a little time to learn some new tricks, so go take a rest.

Communication: It has gotten to the point that people don't want to talk with each other, and it's clear to you that no one wants to take advantage of your skills. Why bother?

Empathy: Nobody seems to care about anyone's feelings, and you have no energy left for keeping an open, upbeat attitude. Go sit and sulk.

Approachability: You've been there for everyone as things have fallen apart, and you have no more welcoming left in you! So say good-bye.

Dependability: It is obvious to you that nothing and nobody can be relied on. No one is coming to meetings, and no one wants to volunteer to keep things going. You're giving up.

Risk Taking: For a long time, you have been encouraging people to look at things differently and to let go of old ways. With the way things are now, you just don't feel like pushing new ideas anymore. Let it go.

Vision and Leadership: You are the only ones left; it's up to you to pick up all the slack. What are you going to do? How will you keep it together?

_____   _____

_____

_____

_____   _____

_____

_____

_____   _____

_____

_____

From *Teambuilding with Teens: Activities for Leadership, Decision Making, and Group Success* by Mariam G. MacGregor, M.S., copyright © 2008. Free Spirit Publishing Inc., Minneapolis, MN; www.freespirit.com. This page may be photocopied for individual, classroom, and group work only. For all other uses, call 800-735-7323.

Communication

Teams Building

Snowflake

Traveling Teams

Our Community

Puzzle

Teams Building

(30–35 MINUTES)

Designed to encourage discussion of communication, teamwork, and the importance of each person's role, this activity reinforces the process of working as a team as much as the outcome of the group's efforts. Teens are divided into groups of three who work together in two phases. First, each team designs and creates a structure with marshmallows and toothpicks, unaware that they are building it for another team to duplicate. Then the teams must work to replicate the design another team has made, relying on assigned roles for each group member. It is in this second phase that the most significant learning takes place. You will need a room with ample space for several small groups of teens to work independently of the other groups.

GOALS

Participants will:

- learn to work as a team using specific resources and instructions
- clarify challenges that can arise even with an obvious group goal in mind
- strengthen communication and teamwork skills

MATERIALS NEEDED

- Bags of multicolored marshmallows, enough to give each team of 3 teens 40 marshmallows
- Multicolored toothpicks, enough to give each team of 3 teens 40 toothpicks
- Plastic resealable sandwich bags, one for each team
- One chair for each team; *optional*—additional chairs or tables

GETTING READY

Organize the marshmallows, toothpicks, and sandwich bags. Place a row of chairs (one chair for each team) at the front of the room with the seats toward the wall and the backs toward the room. If possible, set up other chairs or tables for teams to use as bases for their structures, allowing space so other teams will not observe their work. (If necessary, teens can build on the floor.)

Determine how you will divide your larger group into smaller teams of three members each.

ACCOMMODATIONS

For groups where teens have physical challenges requiring crutches or a wheelchair, this activity can still be conducted as described. The space used for building the structures will need to be larger to accommodate movement. The path from the hidden structures of the other teams and their workspace must be clear of obstacles. For teens with limited manual dexterity, the activity will be challenging; they may require assistance handling the toothpicks and marshmallows.

Setting the Stage

When teams begin this project, they tend to build with creativity but not malice. They don't know another team will need to replicate their structure, and so they focus only on coming up with their own unique, interesting design. While they usually start with an attitude of competition (even though you don't *say* it's a competition), teens soon discover that their success won't be measured by beating the other teams but will depend upon the work their group does to achieve the goal. The activity is most effective when you allow these discoveries to play out naturally.

Activity

Divide your group into teams with three members each. Ask each small team to find a location in the room—away from the row of chairs at the front of the room—where they will be able to work on a project without other teams seeing their work. Set up the activity by saying:

> I am giving you some raw materials—marshmallows and toothpicks—which you will use to put together a structure. Your structure can be two-dimensional or three-dimensional and as unique as you wish. You may use no more than 20 marshmallows and 20 toothpicks for your design. Use the toothpicks whole; do not bend or break them. I'm also giving you a sandwich bag. Each time you add a marshmallow or toothpick to your structure, place an identically colored marshmallow or toothpick in the bag. Be sure that your bag contains the exact items that your structure has. While you are building, keep your structure out of the other teams' view. You'll have 5 minutes to build your structure. Have fun and be creative.

Pass out marshmallows, toothpicks, and sandwich bags. Allow the teams 5 minutes to build their structures.

Walk around the room to keep participants on task and to remind them to place identical materials in the bag. Also remind them to keep their structures away from the view of the other teams. When everyone has completed a structure, say:

> Great! Now that you've finished your constructions, each person on your team will serve your team in a specific role: Explainer, Messenger, or Builder. Once you've decided each person's role, I'll tell you more about what is going to happen.

Allow teams 1–2 minutes to assign the roles, and then continue:

> Here's how you'll do the next part of the activity. First, the Explainer from each team will carry the team's structure, and the bag of matching materials, to the front of the room and place them on one of the chairs. Explainers, as you walk up, keep your design hidden from the other teams. After setting it down, remain standing with your face toward the rest of the group and your back toward the back of the chair. Avoid looking at the other teams' designs.

Allow 1–2 minutes for the Explainers to place the structures and bags on a chair. Then say:

> Here's how the rest of the activity will go. Explainers from each team are going to select a structure *other* than the one their team built by moving to a chair with another team's construction. Only one team's Explainer will be at each chair. When I say so, Explainers, you will go to another chair, *without* looking at the structure, still keeping your back to the chairs. After you do this, wait to turn around to look at the design until I say "Start."
>
> At that moment, team Messengers will come forward to get the bags of toothpicks and marshmallows to take back to the Builders. Builders, you'll stay where you are. Your job will be to build a new structure identical to the model your Explainer has

selected at the front of the room. You won't see the model, though. The Messenger will go between you and the Explainer and get information to help you do your job. The Explainer must do her or his best job of telling the Messenger what the design looks like, including the color and where all the marshmallows and toothpicks are. The Messenger must do the best job he or she can do to tell the Builder what the Explainer said. Builders, you will use the information the Messenger delivers to build the identical structure at your table. Builders can ask Messengers questions about information needed from the Explainers. Messengers can keep going back and forth as much as necessary.

Again, these are the basic rules: The Explainer is the *only* one who can see the model that the team is trying to copy. The Messenger *cannot* look at the design; neither can the Builder. The Builder is the only one who can touch the structure or the raw materials while building it. The Messenger is the only one who can speak to the Explainer and the Builder. Builders and Explainers may not talk to one another.

If your group has a high level of rapport and you want additional challenge, set a rule that the Messenger can't see what the Builder is building until the end. If applying this rule, the Messenger must provide information from the Explainer without being able to point to or correct the Builder. If choosing to add this rule, state it now.

Ask if there are questions. Then say:

You have 10 minutes. Start! Messengers, come forward to get the materials and information to bring to the Builders.

Monitor the groups as they begin the process and remind Builders and Messengers that it's okay to ask questions. Walk around the room to assure that each person is playing the assigned role and not overstepping the limits.

The back-and-forth process continues, with the Messenger taking as many trips as necessary between the Builder and Explainer, until the team feels confident that they've built an identical design. Once all the teams feel they've re-created the structures and time is up, ask all three members from each team to get together with both structures to see how well they completed the task. Then bring the teams together as a larger group to discuss the

"Talk About It" questions and apply what they learned within their teams.

Talk About It

This is a lively activity, and while each team had the same goal, it's likely that they all worked very differently together. Take 10–15 minutes to discuss how the small teams worked together and what they experienced and learned about communication from this activity. Use questions like the following:

- **After building your structures the first time, what was your reaction when you realized what you would do next?**

- **Describe what it was like to be the Explainer, the Messenger, or the Builder. Which role do you think was the most challenging? Why?**

- **If this had been an exceptionally important task to communicate about, how well would your team have done? What would need to change for your team to be more effective as communicators?**

- **Was there any time during this activity when you wanted to cheat, maybe by peeking at the model or in some other way? Why did or didn't you do this?** (Relate this to real-life situations where people are given clear instructions on what is or isn't acceptable in the process of completing a task.)

- **In what ways does this activity relate to how rumors and gossip spread? Were there times when you found yourself doubting the information being communicated to you? If it were a rumor going around, how would you have responded?**

Wrapping Up

Ask teens to observe the specific roles they play in their circle of friends or in other groups they belong to. Remind them to look at the interconnectedness and communication among people in different roles and how groups have successfully established those roles. Encourage teens to write in their notebooks or journals about accomplishing group goals, communicating, and working as a team while restricted to specific rules and roles.

Snowflake

- Communication skills • Listening skills

(20 MINUTES)

This is a quick activity for highlighting the importance of clear communication and active listening in order to accurately express ideas and instructions or receive messages from others. After hearing the same directions for creating a simple paper snowflake, teens discover that the individual results can vary considerably.

GOALS

Participants will:

- identify ways that messages can be misinterpreted
- strengthen communication skills

- recognize the value of being able to use different communication and listening techniques to deliver and receive messages

MATERIALS NEEDED

- One 8½" x 11" sheet of white paper for each participant

Activity

Pass out a piece of paper to each participant. Tell teens that you want them to follow the directions you are about to give without asking questions and without paying attention to or working with others in the group. Then give the following directions quickly, without clarifying exactly what you mean:

1. **Fold the paper in half and tear off a top corner.**
2. **Fold it in half again and tear off the top corner.**
3. **Fold it in half again and tear off the left corner.**
4. **Rotate the paper to the right three times and tear off the bottom corner.**
5. **Fold it in half again and tear off the middle piece.**

67

Instruct the group to now unfold the paper and compare their snowflakes with those around them. They will find that their snowflakes may or may not match others.

Talk About It

Discuss the importance of communicating clearly, as illustrated by the different ways participants interpreted the same instructions. Ask questions like the following:

- **Why is it that even though everyone received the same directions, not everyone had the same outcome? What would have changed if you could have asked questions?**

- **Have you ever told someone one thing only to have the person hear and do something different? What happened, and how did you deal with it?**

- **If you are the leader of a group, what steps can you take to make sure that others clearly understand what you've told them?**

- **How can you improve your communication skills when it becomes obvious that others are seeing things differently than you intended?**

Wrapping Up

If space allows, hang the snowflakes up in your room to remind teens of the importance of communicating clearly and of the different ways messages can be received. If space is limited, suggest that teens keep their snowflakes in their notebooks or journals as a reminder about the importance of clear communication and dialogue.

Traveling Teams

- Teamwork and group dynamics
- Communication skills • Building trust

(45 MINUTES)

Working as a team and building trust within that team go hand in hand. In this activity, teens are given the opportunity to rely on others to guide them through an obstacle course. Working together in teams of three, teens take turns being a blindfolded "Traveler" who is guided through the course by the other two teammates.

Even if your group has met together frequently, blindfolded participants generally find themselves outside of their usual comfort zone. You will need a room or an outdoor area with ample space for setting up and moving along the obstacle course.

GOALS

Participants will:

- build teamwork skills that transfer from small groups to large groups
- strengthen communication skills
- establish a sense of trust and recognize how to continue building trust as a group

MATERIALS NEEDED

- Cloth strips or bandanas (for blindfolds), one for each participant
- Objects for building an obstacle course, such as chairs, desks, hula hoops, balls, collapsible play tunnels, yarn or string, or other materials

GETTING READY

Move any tables, chairs, or desks out of the way to create an open area for movement. Around the room or area, set up an obstacle course that is neither too big nor too complicated. Your goal is to provide enough of a challenge while still allowing small groups to get through the course (three times per group) without feeling overwhelmed or intimidated. Create an area throughout the obstacle course that can be identified as the walking path and that is free of impediments. Allow space between obstacles. You may want to have some teens assist with setting up the course ahead of time.

If conducting this activity outdoors, choose a location where teens can participate in an uninhibited and completely trusting way—that is, where they won't be self-conscious that others might watch from windows or walk through or modify the course. Incorporate indoor objects with natural outdoor elements such as trees, benches, or walls.

Have a blindfold available for each teen and determine how you will divide your larger group into smaller teams of three members each.

ACCOMMODATIONS

For groups where teens have physical challenges requiring crutches or a wheelchair, this activity is challenging, but it can be done. The members of the group will need to work together to set ground rules for accommodating teens with challenges without compromising the goals of the activity. In this case, the obstacle course needs to be designed so teens can make it around any barriers without physical interference. As an alternative to the obstacle course described, you can set up a path using yarn or string strung tautly between chairs, sturdy construction cones, trees, or other types of posts. Using the twine as a road map to guide teen Travelers allows those with physical challenges to serve as guides, too. They can hold onto the line and, as long as they can see, can guide the Travelers around the room without encountering unexpected obstacles.

This type of format can be used for teens with sight limitations as well. By using the string to guide the path, teens can hold onto it and move through the course safely.

Setting the Stage

Trust-building activities are important to incorporate into group experiences, whether the group has met a few times or has been together for a while. By their very nature, such exercises call on group members to accept and face personal challenges. Because this activity involves the use of blindfolds—an experience that some teens may be uncomfortable with—you will want to allow teens to participate as blindfolded Travelers by choice. A concept that can help you facilitate this is "Challenge by Choice" or CbC.

CbC is an approach to facilitated learning endorsed by Project Adventure (www.pa.org), a nonprofit education and training organization known for its innovative experiential education approach. CbC encourages individuals to learn to set activity goals that offer the right degree of personal challenge to improve skills and contribute to the group, rather than setting goals that are too easy or difficult or contribute nothing. The level of challenge depends on the individual. An example of CbC for this activity might be that a teen who is anxious about wearing a blindfold can offer to participate as the Traveler by wearing it through at least half of the obstacle course, with agreement from the small group that she or he can remove the blindfold at any time after that.

Some teens may be too uncomfortable taking personal risks to engage fully in the activity. With this in mind, explain the CbC concept to the group, saying that you expect an attitude of CbC from all members of each group. When you acknowledge their hesitancy ahead of time, teens are likely to appreciate your sensitivity to their perspectives and, in turn, may be more likely to participate to a greater extent than they otherwise would. By openly establishing expectations and choices in this way, you also set the tone for peers to be sensitive to others in their group.

Activity

Before explaining the activity, divide the large group into smaller groups of three. Pass out a blindfold to each participant. Then explain the activity like this:

> **In front of you is an obstacle course. As a large group, you will first determine the path that you think this obstacle course follows. Then, in your small groups, you'll work together as teams to get through the course. This is not a competition. Instead, when working in your small groups, two of you will have full sight and one will be blindfolded. The sighted members are responsible for safely and successfully guiding the blindfolded Traveler through the obstacle course. Each of you gets the opportunity to be the Traveler, so once you finish guiding one person through you'll switch roles and guide the next person through. This means you'll go through the course three times.**

Take time at this point to explain "Challenge by Choice" (see "Setting the Stage"), letting groups know they can determine together how each member will meet the challenge of traveling through the obstacle course. Then continue:

Even though the obstacle course is the same for everyone, in your small groups I want you to determine what the course represents to you. For example, you may imagine that it's another planet or that you're moving across the ocean. Or, it may be something more realistic such as moving through the process to get your next group project off the ground. No matter what the course represents, as the guides are leading the Traveler, create a story for each obstacle or task you must get through. (Offer examples: Walking around the table can represent a rock in the way, or going down the slide can symbolize easy passage from point A to point B. Your examples will depend on how you've set up your obstacle course and what ideas you want your group to focus on as they undertake the course.)

When you're the guide, it's your job to describe the surroundings with as much detail as possible including sounds, smells, colors, or other movement. Focus on communicating well within your own small group—don't be distracted by the techniques other groups are using. Your journey through the course is to be done at walking speed, and guides are responsible for paying attention to where other groups are around your Traveler. Are there any questions?

Allow 3–5 minutes to answer any questions. Then ask small groups to line up in a centralized area, with the first Travelers in each group putting on their blindfolds to begin the process. Once the travels begin, space each group out by several minutes so there is safe flow when proceeding through the course. When a group has made it through the course, ask them to walk around the outside to return to the beginning, ready to start with a new Traveler. In addition to indicating when teams should start the course, you will want to pay attention to what is happening on the course to prevent groups from running into each other and to make sure teams are maintaining the safety of their blindfolded Travelers.

When everyone has participated as the Traveler in a small group, congratulate participants and encourage them to acknowledge their success before bringing everyone together to talk about their experience and apply what they learned.

Talk About It

Take 10 minutes to talk about the activity. Consider these discussion questions related to your group's experience:

- **What did the journey through the path represent to your group? What did some of the obstacles stand for?**
- **Did you trust your team members before doing the activity? Why or why not? Do you trust them more after completing the obstacle course? Less? Explain.**
- **How successful was your small team in working together to get through the course? Were there things you would change if you did it again? If so, what are they and why?**
- **When you were blindfolded, how well do you think your group communicated? When you were the guide, how well do you think you communicated? When there were communication breakdowns, what happened? How did your group deal with any frustration that arose?**
- **What communication skills did you rely on when you were the Traveler? What other skills did you rely on?** (In the case where teens in the group have sight impairments or other sensory disabilities, ask if there were any differences between participating in the experience and navigating obstacles on a daily basis.)
- **If trust doesn't exist in a team, or if a team's trust has been broken, how can you work to develop it? Why is trust important for teams?**

Wrapping Up

Encourage teens to write in their notebooks or journals about the experience of allowing themselves to trust their teammates, about working together as a team to move through the obstacle course, and about the value or challenge of developing trust in a group.

Our Community

LEARNING CONCEPTS

- Understanding others • Personal values and diversity
- Sharing and communicating with others • Getting to know others

(25–45 MINUTES)

This interactive activity encourages individuals within the group to learn about each other in a one-on-one way. Teens are given a handout with 30 squares on it that describe members of different communities. As in a bingo game, participants try to fill in squares, in this case with the signatures of people who see themselves as belonging to the communities described. Teens move around the room, signing other people's handouts and inviting them to fill in theirs. When the forms are completed, they will have a different person's name in each signed box. You can use this activity with unlimited numbers of participants, since there are plenty of spots on the handout and everyone doesn't need to sign everyone else's card.

Use the activity as an icebreaker or during times when you're discussing issues of diversity. Because teens move around and touch base with many group members individually, there is less risk involved than in sitting in a circle disclosing information to everyone at once. A variation allows your group to use a blank form to create their own community categories. This may be especially appropriate if working with groups who share unique needs, such as teen parents or students in residential treatment, or in settings where gang involvement is prevalent, where multiple religious or immigrant groups are present, or where other particular conditions may shape participants' sense of community.

GOALS

Participants will:

- learn how different facets of their personality are connected
- learn more about how others see themselves
- identify similarities and differences in the group to determine ways to strengthen how the group works together

MATERIALS NEEDED

- Fine-point markers or colored pencils, a different color for each participant
- Handout: "Our Community" (page 75)
- *Optional*—Handout: Customizable "Our Community" form (page 76; see "Variation")

GETTING READY

Make a copy of the "Our Community" handout for each teen, or prepare and copy your own handout using the customizable form. (If you want teens to fill in their own descriptions, make copies of the blank customizable form and review the instructions for the "Variation" before conducting the activity.) Place the markers or colored pencils in a central location, accessible to everyone.

Activity

Pass out a copy of the "Our Community" handout to each teen. Ask each person to choose one marker or colored pencil to use for the entire activity. Before participants begin writing on the form, explain the goal of the activity, using words like these:

As an individual, you're part of many different groups, all of which make you the person you are. Members of this group come from lots of communities: only children, athletes, left-handed people—the list could be very long! This handout highlights some of these different communities. You are going to walk around and try to connect with as many people in the room as possible, one person at a time. When you meet a person, say hello to each other and then ask, "What community do you identify with?" or "What box describes you?" You'll sign just one box on the person's sheet, and he or she will sign just one on yours; then you'll each move on to other people. Even though you will identify more closely with some descriptions, be sure to write your name in a different box on each sheet instead of signing the same box over and over. This may mean that you will stretch beyond the ways most people know you to show some of the other characteristics that make you who you are. Please use the same marker or pencil throughout the activity, so at the end you'll be able to clearly recognize each person's "communities" by the color of the writing.

VARIATION

You may wish to have teens write their own descriptions to represent how they perceive the different communities they belong to. If so, introduce the activity using language like this:

As an individual, you're part of many different groups, all of which make you the person you are. Members of this group come from lots of communities. (Mention some obvious and less-obvious categories that fit members of your group, You might say, "Take me, for example. I'm Russian, Jewish, bilingual, an oldest son, and a baseball fan. These are all descriptions of communities I'm part of along with other people who are Russian, or Jewish, or bilingual, or oldest sons, or fans of baseball.") Then continue:

The list of communities you belong to could be very long! This handout is blank so you can write in descriptions of the different communities that make up this group. Here's how you'll do it: You are going to walk around and try to connect with as many people in the room as possible, one person at a time. When you meet a person, say hello to each other and then ask, "What community do you identify with?" or "What group do you belong to that describes you in some way?" For each person you meet, you'll write the name of a group or community you're a part of and then sign your name. Write this in one box. The other person will do the same on your sheet. For example, you might write that you're from a particular culture or that you like a certain kind of music, celebrate certain holidays, speak a particular language, do or don't eat meat, and so forth. (Use examples that are relevant to the group you're working with.) **Be sure to write something different on each sheet instead of writing the same information about yourself over and over. This may mean that you will stretch beyond the ways most people know you to show some of the other characteristics that make you who you are. Please use the same marker or pencil throughout the activity, so at the end you'll be able to clearly recognize each person's "communities" by the color of the writing.**

Take 1–2 minutes to answer questions, and then have teens begin. After everyone has connected with others in the group and the handouts are completely filled in, bring the group together to share what they learned about others by discussing the "Talk About It" questions.

Talk About It

Take 5–10 minutes to talk about the diversity in the group and the experience of finding out more about each other while doing the "Our Community" activity. You may want to consider these discussion questions:

- **What did you learn about the different communities people in your group are a part of? Are there any that a majority of you belong to? What does this tell you about your similarities and differences?** (Make a point of looking together at the different colors that show up in each of the boxes. If you see interesting patterns—such as that person A and person B identify with very different communities, yet share similar ones—comment on this and encourage teens to look for commonalities that stand out. It may be helpful to go around the room, having teens tell what color marker they used and comment on patterns they now see about themselves that they hadn't been aware of until seeing the "color-coded" qualities on the handouts.)

- **How comfortable were you telling people something that they may not have known about you? Explain.**

- **Were there any communities you're a part of that you wanted to (sign your name to/write on the handout) more than once? Why or why not?**

- **Were there any communities that most people indicated they are part of but that you didn't? What does it feel like not to be part of these communities?**

- **Beyond this activity, what communities feel the most comfortable to you? What is it like for you when you're in a community where you don't feel you share anything in common with others? Explain.**

- **How does this group make others feel welcome? If people don't feel welcome, what needs to be different in the group so they do?**

If conducting the "Variation," also ask:

Were there any communities or groups that you identify with but that you didn't write on anyone's sheet? Why didn't you write these down?

Wrapping Up

At the end of the group meeting, and if space allows, display the handouts on the wall or board so others can view and read them when the group gathers again. Alternatively or at a later point, teens may want to take their completed handouts home or place them in their notebooks or journals.

Our Community

Invite individual group members to sign their names in the boxes that represent them. Each person may sign only one box. You will also be signing your name to boxes on other group members' handouts. Try to write your name in a different box on each sheet you sign.

I am a vegetarian	I am an only child	I am an athlete	I know or have known all of my grandparents	My religion is important to me	I have a part-time job
I have never been camping	I have lots of sisters and brothers	I have a pet	I am a boy	I speak more than one language fluently	I play a musical instrument
I will be a first-generation graduate	I am from a unique culture	I am a girl	I moved here from a different country	I have a family member in the armed forces	I enjoy reading
I volunteer regularly	I was born in this community	I have a nontraditional family	I am or have been a Girl Scout or Boy Scout	I make friends easily	I am left-handed
I have a special talent that others don't have	I celebrate a unique holiday	I know how to cook	Someone close to me has died	I am the oldest child in my family	I like _____ (style) music

From *Teambuilding with Teens: Activities for Leadership, Decision Making, and Group Success* by Mariam G. MacGregor, M.S., copyright © 2008. Free Spirit Publishing Inc., Minneapolis, MN; www.freespirit.com. This page may be photocopied for individual, classroom, and group work only. For all other uses, call 800-735-7323.

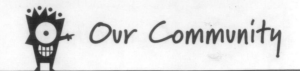 Our Community

Invite individual group members to choose a blank box, write a description of a community they are part of, and sign their names. Each person may write in only one box. You will also be filling in boxes on other group members' handouts. Try to write about a different community each time you write on someone's handout.

From *Teambuilding with Teens: Activities for Leadership, Decision Making, and Group Success* by Mariam G. MacGregor, M.S., copyright © 2008. Free Spirit Publishing Inc., Minneapolis, MN; www.freespirit.com. This page may be photocopied for individual, classroom, and group work only. For all other uses, call 800-735-7323.

Puzzle

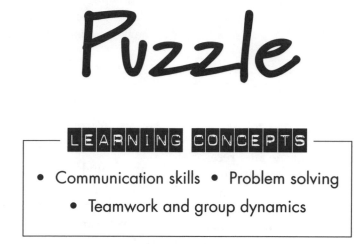

(**25–35 MINUTES**)

This activity emphasizes problem solving via different methods of communication. Teens work in pairs, with one person guiding the other in an attempt to put together a puzzle. The pairs try to accomplish the goal in three different ways, twice with limitations on how they communicate, and finally with as much back-and-forth conversation necessary. Typically, when the partners can communicate freely, they solve the puzzle more quickly than when restrictions are in place. You will need ample floor space for partners to work independently of other paired teams.

GOALS

Participants will:

- learn to work as a team using limited resources and no verbal communication
- clarify challenges that can arise even with an obvious group goal in mind
- strengthen nonverbal communication skills

MATERIALS NEEDED

- Card stock or other stiff paper
- Scissors
- Resealable plastic sandwich bags, one for each pair of teens (if conducting the "Variation," two bags for each pair)
- Folder or envelope to hold 8½" x 11" paper
- Handout: "Puzzle Key" (page 80)

GETTING READY

On card stock or other stiff paper, make one copy of the "Puzzle Key" handout for each pair of teens. For each handout, cut out the puzzle pieces along the lines and place the pieces in a resealable plastic bag. Seal the bag. Repeat until you have half as many sets of puzzle pieces as there are teens in your group.

On regular copy paper, make one copy of the "Puzzle Key" handout for each pair of teens. This is the master design for the puzzle, so don't cut these copies up; place them in a folder where the completed design cannot be seen.

(If you are conducting the "Variation," make two sets of the cut-up puzzle pieces in plastic bags for each set of partners *instead* of copying and setting aside intact "Puzzle Key" sheets. In this case you will have a bag with puzzle pieces for each person in the group.)

Organize the room so that there is ample space on the floor where teens can sit back-to-back in pairs.

Activity

Teens work in pairs in this three-stage activity. First, one partner tries to correctly assemble a puzzle after receiving instructions from the other partner and without being able to ask questions. Next, the person attempts the same task, but this time is able to ask yes-and-no questions. In the third and final attempt, the two partners are able to talk freely. You'll discuss "Talk About It" questions after all three attempts have been made.

Partner up the teens; have each pair identify who will be Partner "A" and who will be Partner "B." They will maintain these roles throughout the activity. Once they have identified their roles, have them sit on the floor, back-to-back. They are to remain in this position throughout the process, each unable to see what the other is doing. Explain the activity process by saying:

I will give each of you a puzzle in some form. "A" partners, you are going to receive a copy of the completed puzzle—this is the puzzle's answer key. You are to keep this out of Partner "B's" view. "B" partners, you will receive the puzzle pieces in a plastic bag. Staying exactly where you are, with your backs to each other, Partner "B" will put the puzzle together following instructions from Partner "A." Each pair of partners is a team. Each team will work independently of the other teams. This means that all "A" partners need to make sure *none* of the "B" partners sees the key to the puzzle.

Once the activity begins, you will have three tries to finish the puzzle. Each try has different rules. The goal in all three attempts is for "A" partners to communicate to "B" partners what they need to know in order to put the puzzle together so it matches the finished puzzle key.

Pass out the puzzle keys to all "A" partners and the bags of puzzle pieces to all "B" partners. Then continue:

Now that you have the puzzles, here's what you'll do first: Partner "A" will explain to Partner "B" how to put the puzzle together. For this first attempt, only Partner "A" can speak. Partner "B" cannot speak or ask questions. You have 5 minutes.

Walk around the room making sure that "B" partners remain quiet and cannot see the answer keys held by any "A" partners. Call time at 5 minutes, regardless of whether teams have finished their puzzles. Then instruct the group for the second attempt by saying:

It's time to try again. Partner "B," if you don't think you solved the puzzle the first time, you'll have another chance now. If you do think you solved it, Partner "A" will rotate (turn) the answer key so the puzzle design is different this time. Partner "A" will again tell Partner "B" how to put the puzzle together. This time, Partner "B" can ask questions that Partner "A" can answer *only* by saying yes or no. Again, you have 5 minutes.

Walk around the room making sure that partners are asking and answering only yes-and-no questions. Call time at 5 minutes, regardless of whether teams have finished their puzzles. Then instruct the group for the final attempt by saying:

Once again, if you think Partner "B" solved the puzzle, then Partner "A" should rotate the key again so the puzzle design is different from both earlier tries. Partner "A," you're still trying to help Partner "B" solve the puzzle. Although neither partner can see what the other is doing, you can both talk freely through this attempt. You have 5 minutes.

This attempt is likely to go quickly and smoothly; still, call time at 5 minutes regardless of whether teams have finished their puzzles. Then allow partners to look together at the key and the final result. Bring teens together in the large group for a "Talk About It" discussion of the learning that took place during all three attempts.

Rather than use an answer key, have "A" partners use puzzle pieces to create their own design and then have "B" partners duplicate it. After each attempt, allow Partner "A" to show Partner "B" his or her design and allow them to compare puzzles. "A" partners will need to put the puzzle together in a different way for each attempt. Otherwise the activity and discussion proceed in the same way, with no questions for the first attempt, yes-and-no questions for the second, and free conversation for the third, followed by the "Talk About It" discussion.

Talk About It

Ask questions like the following to help your group apply what they learned:

- **Describe what it was like to be Partner "A" or Partner "B." When you're part of a different team, which person do you most frequently feel like, "A" or "B"? How does this role work for you? What would you change?**

- **Each time you attempted to accomplish the task, you needed to rely on different communication skills. Explain what you dealt with as partners during each of the different attempts.**

- **What happens to relationships in a group when one person has more information than others? How can members of a group deal with this type of situation?**

- **Can you think of some real-life situations where you were trying to solve a problem but didn't have all the "pieces"—all the information—you needed? What would have changed in that situation if you had received more information or if others had communicated more clearly with you while you tried to solve the problem?**

- **What happens when one person in your group has a specific goal in mind but can't clearly communicate it to the group? How can your group improve the way information is communicated to everyone involved?**

Wrapping Up

Encourage teens to write in their notebooks or journals about team communication and the obstacles, challenges, and insights they experienced or observed.

Extending the Learning

Repeat the activity later, using a more complex puzzle. A fun way to reinforce the leadership learning from this activity can take place if the group gets together at another time, such as for a retreat. Have them work together on a real, larger puzzle; let the communication and problem solving be free flowing. Refer back to the original "Puzzle" activity and the differences in solving puzzles when communication and teamwork roadblocks are imposed.

Do a human-size puzzle with younger students. Have teen mentors create large versions of the puzzle pieces by drawing them on card stock by hand. (The "Puzzle Key" handout can still serve as the answer key.) Once this is done, teen facilitators can divide the younger students into smaller teams of three or four, with one person from each team having clear instructions about what the puzzle should look like. With the guidance of the teen mentors, this person delivers the message the same way Partner "A" did in the original activity, taking three attempts with the same restrictions to guide his or her team to complete the task. An age-appropriate discussion should progress as in the "Talk About It" on this page.

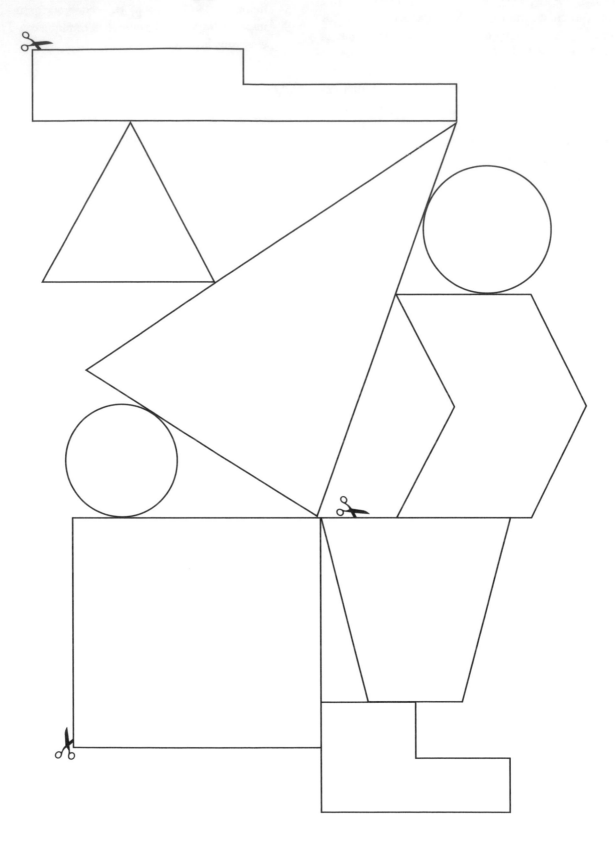

From *Teambuilding with Teens: Activities for Leadership, Decision Making, and Group Success* by Mariam G. MacGregor, M.S., copyright © 2008. Free Spirit Publishing Inc., Minneapolis, MN; www.freespirit.com. This page may be photocopied for individual, classroom, and group work only. For all other uses, call 800-735-7323.

Qualities of Leadership

Campaign Teams

Heroes

Treasure Hunt

The Party

Quote/End Quote

Wise Sayings

Campaign Teams

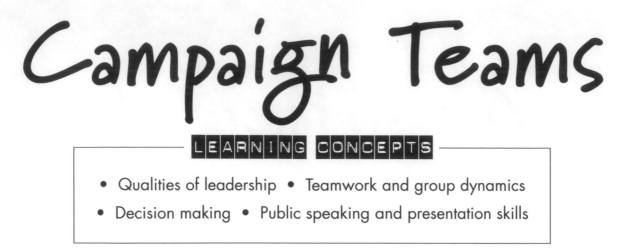

- Qualities of leadership • Teamwork and group dynamics
- Decision making • Public speaking and presentation skills

(TWO MEETINGS, 45–60 MINUTES EACH)

This abbreviated simulation of a campaign for city mayor allows teens to experience firsthand the process of creating a campaign to get a candidate elected. Each of the mock candidates in this exercise has strengths and challenges, and teens must develop a plan for their candidate with these characteristics in mind. The process of designing a winning campaign illustrates the impact stereotypes and personal bias can have on election outcomes. It also highlights many leadership topics in both obvious and subtle ways. Teens' decision-making and communication skills are likely to be challenged, as are their ethical beliefs and their ability to work with a small team toward a common goal. Personal views come into play when people are given profiles of candidates that they may or may not believe in and as they work to establish the sex, ethnicity, age, and family status of their candidates based on the information provided.

The activity is best accomplished using two meeting periods. In the first, teens focus on creating their candidate's full profile and establishing their campaign platform; in the second, they present their campaign speeches, elect a mayor, and talk about the overall experience. You will need ample space to set up tables for each candidate as well as wall space for posters.

GOALS

Participants will:

- gain a broad understanding of the leadership qualities people seek in public leaders
- solve problems and make decisions in the best interest of their group's goal
- learn more about others in the group and how they can work together in light of different perspectives or biases
- practice skills in public speaking and putting together a presentation

MATERIALS NEEDED

- Construction paper, poster board, newsprint, or a roll of banner paper
- Scissors
- Masking tape
- Markers, paints, or crayons

- Small slips of paper and an empty shoe box
- Pen or pencil for each participant
- Handouts: "Profile of Candidate A," "Profile of Candidate B," "Profile of Candidate C," "Profile of Candidate D," and "Profile of Candidate E" (pages 85–89)
- *Optional*—Streamers, magazines and newspapers for cutting out visuals, balloons, other decorative supplies

GETTING READY

Make four or five copies of each handout, enough so that each team's members can have individual copies of their candidate's information. If you have over 20–25 participants, more than one team will need to support a given candidate. This is okay, since it's interesting to see how two different groups develop a candidate based on the same basic information. You may wish to add or change characteristics and information for teens to consider related to the profiles. Make these changes prior to copying the handouts.

Collect the other materials and place them in an area easily accessible to everyone in the group.

Determine how you will divide the large group into smaller teams of four or five teens.

Activity: Part 1

During Part 1, teams are assigned their candidate and use the full activity period to develop the candidate's profile and platform, write a short campaign speech, and create promotional posters to use for Part 2.

Divide the large group into teams of four or five teens and pass out the appropriate candidate profiles to each group. Explain what they're to do by saying:

You've received the basic description of candidates for your city's mayoral election. Each of your groups is a campaign team for one candidate: it's your job to get your candidate elected. First, you need to fully develop your candidate's profile—the person's description, background, and experience—based on the handout you've received. In the time we have today, you will give your person a name and fill in the other missing information on the profile. Then you will select who on your team will take the role of this candidate. You'll formulate a campaign plan to explain why your candidate is the right person for the job, put together promotional posters, and write a 2- to 3-minute campaign speech for your candidate to deliver. The introductions, the campaign speeches, and the election will take place at your next meeting. At that meeting, your team will have 5 minutes to campaign—to get your points across through the candidate's speech and other efforts. You'll be able to display your posters, introduce your candidate to the voters, and use the profile you've completed to tell why she or he is the best person to be mayor. If you want, you can bring in music or even write a song about your candidate—whatever you think will get people excited about voting for him or her. Remember, you will only have a few minutes to get your message across.

Tell groups how much time they have to accomplish their task during the Part 1 meeting time. Respond briefly to questions and then have teams begin their work. Walk around the room to monitor progress and answer any additional questions. Periodically remind groups of how much time is left; when 10 minutes remain, indicate that they need to wrap up their work.

If space allows, permit teams to hang their promotional posters up in the room. Identify a location where they can store any other campaign materials until the next meeting. Conclude Part 1 by saying:

For our next meeting, be prepared to present your campaign and state why your candidate is the best person for the job. Candidates, be prepared to deliver your speeches, and come determined to get elected!

Activity: Part 2

Identify where in the room each team will be located to present their candidate. When teens come into the room, allow them a few minutes to set up their campaign tables and display their posters and other supporting materials, if they have any.

Briefly explain that teams have 5 minutes for their entire presentation and that they are to begin by presenting their candidate's complete profile as they've developed it. After that, their candidate can present the speech. Ask that the audience remain quiet during the presentations. Finally, tell everyone:

> **Pay close attention. After the campaigns you will vote for the city's mayor, and you may *not* vote for your own candidate.** (You may want to explain this variance from standard election practice: in this activity, where the only voters are those on the campaign teams, allowing people to vote for their own candidates would make it likely that the election would end in a tie.)

Monitor closely so every team is given equal time; with five different teams, this process should take 25 minutes. After all of the presentations have been made, pass out the slips of paper along with pens or pencils and conduct the vote. Remind teens that they cannot cast a vote for their own candidate and that they should vote as individuals, not as teams. Collect the votes in the shoe box and enlist the help of one or two teens to count the ballots and verify the winner. Announce the winner and allow a few minutes for the winning candidate and team to cheer and celebrate. Also take a couple of minutes so that each team can acknowledge the other teams. Recognize the hard work of each team and remind participants of good sportsmanship before bringing everyone together as a large group to discuss the activity.

Talk About It

Synthesize the entire process by asking discussion questions like these:

- **What was it like to be assigned a candidate on paper and to make that person become real?**

- **What stereotypes did you have to overcome on behalf of your candidate's background and abilities? Did your candidate have characteristics that you believe were too difficult to overcome? Did everyone agree? Disagree? Were you unable to overlook any troubling characteristics? Explain.**

- **Do you feel your team made good decisions in developing your campaign? Were you at all tempted to do or say anything unethical or dishonest? Explain.**

- **What can you apply to real-life elections from your experience with this imaginary campaign? Do you think it's important to have a variety of candidates to choose from in an election?**

- **Do you think people running for leadership positions should be held to a higher standard than the average person on the street? Why or why not?**

- **Did the best candidate win? Why or why not?**

Wrapping Up

If space allows, have campaign teams hang their posters around the room. Time permitting, consider having the newly elected mayor make a quick winner's speech to thank the campaign team and announce his or her first goals as mayor. You may also want to have teens imagine they are journalists covering the election and suggest they write an article to appear in the local newspaper the next day.

Extending the Learning

Follow an actual election. If you conduct this activity when a real election is taking place locally, nationally, or globally, have teens follow the media coverage of the candidates. Ask each teen to identify a candidate to support. Throughout the campaign, have teens collect information about the candidate from newspapers, magazines, the Internet, and radio and TV advertisements. If possible, contact the campaign managers and ask if teens can interview them about the process of getting their candidate elected.

Show and discuss the classic film *All the King's Men* based on the Pulitzer Prize–winning novel by Robert Penn Warren. Although the movie was remade in 2006, the 1949 version, available in libraries and rental outlets, strongly illustrates how social norms, prejudices, and personal intentions collide during a political campaign and election. Interesting discussions can evolve from seeing that certain discriminatory attitudes such as racism and classism, which existed more openly in 1949, didn't negatively impact a candidate's electibility to the degree that they might today.

Profile of Candidate

A

Name: _____

Age: _____ **Sex:** _____

Family information: _____

Race/ethnicity: _____

Other personal details: _____

Education: High school diploma; left college after two years

Occupation: President of own computer software company; multimillionaire

Leadership experience:

- President of own company (10 years); manages 20 employees who in turn manage a workforce of 400
- Chairperson of National Computer Organization's finance committee
- President of neighborhood association; helped plan a neighborhood safety program
- Volunteer for Big Brothers Big Sisters

Challenges: Felony charge for drug possession (when 18 years old)

Other: _____

From *Teambuilding with Teens: Activities for Leadership, Decision Making, and Group Success* by Mariam G. MacGregor, M.S., copyright © 2008. Free Spirit Publishing Inc., Minneapolis, MN; www.freespirit.com. This page may be photocopied for individual, classroom, and group work only. For all other uses, call 800-735-7323.

Profile of Candidate

B

Name: _____

Age: _____ **Sex:** _____

Family information: _____

Race/ethnicity: _____

Other personal details: _____

Education:

- Earned GED (General Equivalency Degree)
- Completed associate's degree at community college before transferring to the university to finish a bachelor's degree
- Currently pursuing medical degree to become a brain surgeon

Occupation: Registered nurse

Leadership experience:

- Member of nurses' union board
- Active volunteer at local homeless shelter
- Coordinates annual flea market fundraiser for area retirement homes
- Active in his/her faith community

Challenges:

- Vocal supporter of establishing one accepted "official" language across the country
- Is perceived by others who have worked with him/her as "dictatorial" in leadership style

Other: _____

From *Teambuilding with Teens: Activities for Leadership, Decision Making, and Group Success* by Mariam G. MacGregor, M.S., copyright © 2008. Free Spirit Publishing Inc., Minneapolis, MN; www.freespirit.com. This page may be photocopied for individual, classroom, and group work only. For all other uses, call 800-735-7323.

Profile of Candidate

C

Name: _____

Age: _____ **Sex:** _____

Family information: _____

Race/ethnicity: _____

Other personal details: _____

Education: Ph.D. in government and public service from an Ivy League college

Occupation: Stay-at-home parent

Leadership experience:

- Former president of college Graduate Club
- President of college senior class
- Member of community school board
- Coaches a youth soccer team

Challenges:

- Has not worked full time outside the home for five years
- Was caught shoplifting two candy bars at grocery store; finished 40 hours of community service over the past year to complete probation requirements

Other: _____

From *Teambuilding with Teens: Activities for Leadership, Decision Making, and Group Success* by Mariam G. MacGregor, M.S., copyright © 2008. Free Spirit Publishing Inc., Minneapolis, MN; www.freespirit.com. This page may be photocopied for individual, classroom, and group work only. For all other uses, call 800-735-7323.

Profile of Candidate

D

Name: _____

Age: _____ **Sex:** _____

Family information: _____

Race/ethnicity: _____

Other personal details: _____

Education:

- College graduate; C+ grade point average (GPA) at graduation
- Law school graduate; C+ grade point average
- Perfect score on the state bar exam on the first try

Occupation: Attorney

Leadership experience:

- Member of Moot Court in law school
- Writes legal column for local newspaper
- Member of local school board (currently serving second term)

Challenges: Has never voted in any election and once was interested in joining an anti-government activist group

Other: _____

From *Teambuilding with Teens: Activities for Leadership, Decision Making, and Group Success* by Mariam G. MacGregor, M.S., copyright © 2008. Free Spirit Publishing Inc., Minneapolis, MN; www.freespirit.com. This page may be photocopied for individual, classroom, and group work only. For all other uses, call 800-735-7323.

Profile of Candidate

E

Name: _____

Age: _____ **Sex:** _____

Family information: _____

Race/ethnicity: _____

Other personal details: _____

Education: College graduate; A– grade point average (GPA) at graduation

Occupation: Owns a retail store

Leadership experience:

- Previous member of City Council
- Worked on two presidential campaigns
- Chairperson of Retail Managers Association (has been for five years)
- Advisory board member for current city mayor

Challenges: Unknown outside of professional associations; has never done anything newsworthy or out of the ordinary

Other: _____

From *Teambuilding with Teens: Activities for Leadership, Decision Making, and Group Success* by Mariam G. MacGregor, M.S., copyright © 2008. Free Spirit Publishing Inc., Minneapolis, MN; www.freespirit.com. This page may be photocopied for individual, classroom, and group work only. For all other uses, call 800-735-7323.

Heroes

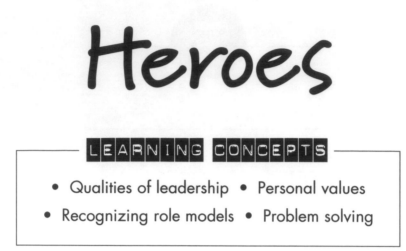

LEARNING CONCEPTS

- Qualities of leadership
- Personal values
- Recognizing role models
- Problem solving

(45 MINUTES)

After a brief discussion of what makes a hero, the full group brainstorms large issues facing society. Then teens work individually, identifying someone they consider to be a hero and imagining that this person is responsible for solving one of the issues, before rejoining the group to discuss thoughts about their role models and what they've learned in the activity. Although it is quite simple, the exercise can evoke lengthy discussions about what people look for in role models and what it takes for someone to be a hero to someone else. This is a great activity for teen mentors to use with younger children.

GOALS

Participants will:

- identify personal beliefs that influence the people they respect and admire
- recognize general qualities expected of people perceived as heroes, mentors, role models, or leaders
- learn what others in the group seek and value in people they look up to

MATERIALS NEEDED

- Newsprint or banner paper
- Masking tape
- Markers
- One 8½" x 11" sheet of white or colored paper for each participant
- Fine-point marker or pen for each participant

GETTING READY

Hang several pieces of newsprint or a large sheet of banner paper on a wall where everyone in the group will be able to see it.

Setting the Stage

In today's diverse and chaotic world, the concept of what makes someone a hero continues to change. For some teens and kids, the belief in heroes has disappeared. Depending on the setting and population of teens you're working with, you may find some students are quite negative about the idea of believing in heroes. If this is the outlook of teens in your group, challenge them to suspend disbelief and to imagine they are in a world where everyone has a hero. Encourage participants to think about people they admire and about the feelings that can come with believing in someone who seems greater than life. If useful, tell the group about your own hero and why that person is heroic in your eyes.

Middle and high school teens working with younger students are likely to find it easier to get the younger children to express their ideas about heroes. Even though some of the younger kids may not identify specific heroes, many typically view their parents, grandparents, older siblings or cousins, or other influential people in their lives as heroes.

Activity

To set the tone, begin a discussion about heroes. Some teens may relate better to the term *role model*, so use that term if it opens up the discussion. Ask questions such as these:

- **Do you have a hero? Why or why not?**
- **What characteristics do you look for in a hero?**
- **How do you describe your hero? What makes the person your hero?**
- **What are some differences between real-life heroes and heroes you see in movies, books, or comics?**

Take 5 minutes to have teens share their views. For the next step in the activity, a brief brainstorming session, ask for a volunteer to serve as recorder and keep track of ideas on the newsprint sheets. Then say to the group:

There are many problems facing society. What are some examples of issues that leaders are facing around the world today? For example, close to home, a big issue is _____ _____. (Use a local example of a topic or concern that is pressing and relevant to teens

in your group.) **As you share your examples, the recorder will write them down so we all can see them. What examples come to mind?**

Take 5 minutes for the large group to brainstorm examples of major issues facing the world or local communities today that require problem solving from leaders and others. After brainstorming, pass out paper and pens or fine-point markers. Ask each teen to think of his or her personal hero. Encourage participants to consider famous or relatively unknown individuals (dead or alive), family members, political leaders, authors, artists, athletes—anyone they admire and consider a role model. Tell them to write the name of this hero on their paper and then turn their paper over so no one can see it. Continue the activity, saying:

Look at the list of problems and issues this group brainstormed. Select one problem you feel strongly about. Imagine that your hero has decided to deal with this issue. What would your hero do? On the blank side of your paper, write your thoughts about how you imagine this person would go about solving or dealing with the problem. Keep these questions in mind: How would your hero approach the problem? What resources and skills does your hero have to use? (Offer examples such as relationships, connections, ingenuity, creativity, respect from others, intelligence, money, or visibility.) **What ideas could your hero give to leaders responsible for dealing with the issue? What advice would your hero offer? What would your hero do to get others to help solve the problem?**

Allow 5–10 minutes for participants to write their thoughts. When everyone has completed this step, go around the room and invite individual teens to hold up the paper with their hero's name on it, explain to the group who the person is, and share why that person is their hero. Then ask them how they think the hero would solve the problem. If other teens have the same hero, ask them to present their heroes next, so the group can see similarities and differences in people's ideas about role models and problem-solving approaches. If desired, ask for a new recorder to summarize a list of heroes and the different solutions people identified to issues and problems.

Once everyone has shared the information on their sheets, take some time to discuss the "Talk About It" questions.

Talk About It

Use 10 minutes to bring the activity to a close and to help the group identify any helpful next steps to finding, believing in, or becoming a hero to someone else. Consider these discussion questions:

- Is it hard for you to find a hero? Why or why not?

- Is it important to have a hero? Why or why not? If you don't have a hero, what steps can you take to find one?

- Should we expect heroes to be problem solvers and leaders? Explain.

- Do you believe heroes have answers for difficult situations? Why or why not?

- What can cause you to stop believing in someone as your hero? Explain.

- What happens when heroes don't live up to the expectations others have of them? How can a hero regain people's trust after letting them down or betraying them?

- What would you expect of yourself if someone told you you're a hero to him or her?

Wrapping Up

If space allows, hang up participants' individual sheets about heroes and keep them posted, along with the newsprint, for future meetings. If space doesn't allow, you may want to have a volunteer summarize and type a list of problems and solutions people shared, make photocopies, and pass them out for teens to keep in their notebooks or journals.

Extending the Learning

Arrange to meet a hero. If a teen identifies a hero who is accessible, ask her or him to set up a meeting with the person. You may need to facilitate this process. At the meeting, have the teen present the problem she or he had the hero solving in the activity and discuss it with the person. After having a first-person conversation with their hero, teens can report back to the group about how the person responded. If possible, invite the hero to meet with the group at a later date.

Treasure Hunt

```
LEARNING CONCEPTS
```

- • Qualities of leadership • Communication skills
- • Teamwork and group dynamics • Getting to know others

(35–45 MINUTES)

Different from a scavenger hunt, this activity has teens working with one another to uncover certain clues about their team. As you ask a series of questions, teens share information about themselves and find out more about others, earning points for their responses. The activity is a good icebreaker and also can be used later on to reconnect participants with members of their group.

GOALS

Participants will:

- • share their abilities and skills with others
- • gain awareness of what others bring to the group
- • work together to achieve a goal through communication and low-risk self-disclosure

MATERIALS NEEDED

- • Handouts: "Treasure Hunt Questions" (pages 95–96) and "Treasure Hunt Score Sheet" (page 97)
- • Pencil or pen for each group of 4–5 teens

GETTING READY

Make one copy of the "Treasure Hunt Questions" for yourself. There are 25 questions on the list and room for you to write five more for a total of up to 30 questions. Some of the questions may not fit the experiences of group members, or you may want them to learn specific things about the others in their group. In this case, write any questions of your own and then select a total of 15 questions that are most applicable to your group. Number them on the sheet: these are the 15 questions you will ask participants.

Make enough copies of the "Treasure Hunt Score Sheet" so that every group of four or five participants will have one score sheet.

Read through the activity and then determine how you will divide the large group into smaller teams of either four or five members. Because teams will keep a score based on an equal number of participants, the ideal is for every team to have the same number of members. If there is only a single "extra" person in the large group, you can have that person read the "Treasure Hunt Questions" to the group instead of you. If you have two or three additional people, one option is to have groups with fewer members automatically add another point for each question. Another is to have groups divide their final score totals by the number of members. You may come up with other ways to assure fair distribution of points.

Activity

Divide the large group into small teams and pass out a "Treasure Hunt Score Sheet" and pen or pencil to each team. Ask teams to identify a scorekeeper who will be responsible for tallying the points throughout the activity. Explain the hunt like this:

> You're going on a treasure hunt. The "hunt" is for particular qualities people on your team possess or things they've done. I am going to read a series of questions. For each question, your team earns *one* point for *each* member of your team who "fits" what the question asks. Be honest in answering each question. The scorekeeper needs to tally the score for each question and then tally the overall score for all of them. I'll ask them slowly. Feel free to talk about the questions, because you'll discover new things about the others in your group.

Allow a couple of minutes to answer questions and let teams settle in. If you are conducting this activity with a new group, take a few extra minutes to have members introduce themselves to their teammates.

Read the questions slowly, moving on only when you think all teams have tallied their scores for a given question. Plan to spend about 25–30 minutes asking the questions and allowing teams time to discuss them. When you've read all of your selected questions, ask the teams to calculate their overall score before moving on to the "Talk About It" discussion.

Talk About It

Bring the large group together, but have teens sit with their teammates. Acknowledge the team that had the highest overall score. Then take 5–10 minutes to discuss the activity, drawing out participants' ideas about incorporating what they learned in their small teams into the cooperative workings of the large group. Consider questions like these related to your group's experience:

- What did you learn about others on your team? How diverse is your team? Were there any individuals who responded to all the same questions? Were there any questions where everyone received a point? Where your team received no points? Explain.

- What questions caused the greatest discussion within your team? Explain.

- Which question was the most challenging for your team? Which was the easiest to answer? What can this group do with the information you learned from this activity?

- What was the most interesting response in your group? Explain.

- What questions would you add to this treasure hunt?

Treasure Hunt Questions

At the end of the list that follows, write alternative questions if you wish. Then pick any 15 questions and number them in the boxes in the order you'll read them. Remind the group: **Your team earns *one* point for *each* team member who "fits" what the question asks.**

☐ Who is involved in a club, an activity, *or* a sports team or works in addition to going to school?

☐ Who has spent time volunteering in the community?

☐ Who has spoken up for a cause or an issue even when others didn't support your opinion?

☐ Who is from a different cultural background? (Let teams determine what "different" means.)

☐ Who currently mentors someone, has mentored others, or is being mentored by someone? (*examples:* tutoring, serving as a peer mentor, being a camp counselor or counselor-in-training, being a Big Brother or Big Sister)

☐ Who has confronted someone who has made an inappropriate comment? (*examples:* racist or sexist remarks, unkind jokes, gossip, insults)

☐ Who can correctly name the capital of our state (province)?

☐ Who has chosen not to go along with friends even when they were pressuring you?

☐ Who speaks more than one language?

☐ Who has attended a teen workshop or leadership conference?

☐ Who has ever been nominated or has run for a position to lead others, including for a sports team, a scout or youth group, a school club, or another organized group?

☐ Who has written a letter to the editor or to a member of Congress, mayor, school principal, or another authority?

☐ Who has stood up to a bully, either for yourself or on behalf of someone else?

☐ Who has been involved in a leadership-specific group such as a student council, youth leader program, counselor-in-training program, political campaign team, youth mentoring team, or another group that means a lot to you?

MORE ➜

From *Teambuilding with Teens: Activities for Leadership, Decision Making, and Group Success* by Mariam G. MacGregor, M.S., copyright © 2008. Free Spirit Publishing Inc., Minneapolis, MN; www.freespirit.com. This page may be photocopied for individual, classroom, and group work only. For all other uses, call 800-735-7323.

☐ Who wants to go to college?

☐ Who plays a musical instrument or sings in a choir?

☐ Who is usually the first person to introduce himself or herself when meeting someone new?

☐ Who can close their eyes and say the names of all the others in their team?

☐ Who has voted in an election of any kind? (Offer two points for any team members of legal voting age who have voted in a governmental election.)

☐ Who has won a contest or competition of any kind?

☐ Who is on a youth advisory board either in school or out? (*examples:* advisory board for the city or community council, mayor's commission, school board, or superintendent's office)

☐ Who knows the name of the current mayor, governor, and president (or other appropriate designations)?

☐ Who celebrates a unique holiday? (Let teams determine what "unique" means.)

☐ Who has ever met a well-known leader from this community or beyond?

☐ Who has ever said thank you to a teacher, law-enforcement officer, principal, mentor, or another person who has made a positive difference in the lives of kids and teens?

Write alternative questions here:

☐ _____

☐ _____

☐ _____

☐ _____

☐ _____

From *Teambuilding with Teens: Activities for Leadership, Decision Making, and Group Success* by Mariam G. MacGregor, M.S., copyright © 2008. Free Spirit Publishing Inc., Minneapolis, MN; www.freespirit.com. This page may be photocopied for individual, classroom, and group work only. For all other uses, call 800-735-7323.

Treasure Hunt Score Sheet

Team Points for Each Question

1. _____

2. _____

3. _____

4. _____

5. _____

6. _____

7. _____

8. _____

9. _____

10. _____

11. _____

12. _____

13. _____

14. _____

15. _____

Total Combined Team Points

_____
Add points from questions 1 and 2

_____
Add points from question 3

_____
Continue to add points from each question

_____

_____

_____

_____

_____

_____

_____

_____

_____

_____
Total score of all questions

From *Teambuilding with Teens: Activities for Leadership, Decision Making, and Group Success* by Mariam G. MacGregor, M.S., copyright © 2008. Free Spirit Publishing Inc., Minneapolis, MN; www.freespirit.com. This page may be photocopied for individual, classroom, and group work only. For all other uses, call 800-735-7323.

The Party

- Recognizing individual strengths of group members
- Understanding others • Group warm-up

(35–45 MINUTES)

Teens write their strengths on small slips of paper, put them into balloons, and blow up the balloons. One by one the balloons are popped to reveal what each person brings to the "party." As the group learns about the unique talents each person has to offer, the information is transferred onto a large wall banner so people can see all of their strengths together.

"The Party" makes for a fun, low-risk icebreaker that helps set the tone for positive team dynamics;

it's also a good activity to use if a group has been working together for some time and needs a refresher on what people can contribute and how the group can work well together. The simplicity of this activity allows it to be used with a wide range of ages, from older to younger teens, and it's a fun one for teen mentors to use when working with younger groups.

GOALS

Participants will:

- identify how a new or existing team wants to work together
- learn how individual members view themselves as part of the group
- learn how to recognize strengths in order to get the most from every member of the group

MATERIALS NEEDED

- Large sheet of banner paper
- Marker
- Masking tape
- Medium-sized balloons, one or more for each participant

- Pens, pencils, or fine-point markers, one for each participant
- Small slips of paper, several for each participant
- Sturdy wooden toothpicks with pointed ends
- *Optional*—Plain 8½" x 11" paper (see "Wrapping Up" on page 99)

GETTING READY

On the banner paper, draw a large bunch of balloons, one for each teen in your group. Hang the banner on the wall in a location where it can be seen by all.

Clear an area in the room where the group can sit in a circle with space in the middle for a pile of blown-up balloons.

Activity

Ask teens to sit in a circle in the area you've designated for the activity. Pass out a pen, pencil, or fine-point marker and at least one slip of paper to each participant, along with a balloon. Let participants know that they should wait to blow up their balloons. Explain the activity using words like these:

> You've all been invited to a party. It's a kind of potluck, but instead of bringing food to share, you're bringing yourself and the strengths you believe you contribute to this group. For example, you may be a creative thinker, or very organized, or able to keep others motivated. On the slip(s) of paper you have, you'll write down the strengths or talents that you bring to the group "party." Once you've written these down, carefully put the slip(s) of paper into your balloon, blow it up, tie it off, and put it in the middle of the circle.

Allow 5 minutes for this part of the activity. When everyone is done, invite a teen to start the "popping" process by picking a balloon from the pile, popping it with a toothpick, and reading the slip(s) inside. After a slip has been read, ask the author to step forward, share a little more, and then write his or her name and strength in a balloon on the wall poster. This person becomes the next one to select a balloon from the pile, pop it, and read the slip. The process is noisy, but fun! Continue until all the balloons have been popped and everyone's names and strengths are written on the wall banner.

When this is complete, bring the activity to closure and allow 1–2 minutes for participants to settle down before discussing the "Talk About It" questions.

VARIATION

Conduct the activity without using balloons. Instead, ask teens, one by one, to step up to the banner and write their name and strengths in one of the balloons. Initially, have teens fill in just one balloon each, so the banner isn't too massive. You can add more balloons if space allows or if teens want to write more than what fits into the existing balloons.

This variation is more effective for a group that already has a good deal of rapport. With newly formed groups, some participants may find it intimidating to talk about their perceived strengths to others, so filling and popping the balloons adds a dimension of fun that helps bring down personal barriers. For more established groups, focusing directly on the banner allows the group to ask questions as participants fill in and talk about their strengths, prompting deeper discussion from the start of the activity.

After everyone has filled in a balloon on the banner, continue with the "Talk About It" discussion.

Talk About It

Take 5–10 minutes to discuss how the group can use the information they've gained from hearing everyone share their strengths. Consider discussion questions like these:

- How can what you've learned from others be used in the future to improve the way this group works together?

- Are there any people who you think overlooked one of their strengths? Who? What is the strength? (If you wish, and you don't feel you're putting that person on the spot, you may want to ask the individual: Did you know others view this as one of your strengths? Do you agree that it is? Why did you overlook it?)

- How can you make the most of strengths and talents of group members and still allow everyone a chance to try new things or use new talents?

- Imagine the group was going to assign official jobs for each member. Based on the strengths people shared, what roles do you think people should have?

- Is the group missing any strengths? What are they and how can you build them? What if you can't? How can you overcome not having certain strengths or prevent the lack of them from becoming a group weakness?

Wrapping Up

If space allows, keep the banner hanging in the room for future meetings. It can remind members of everyone's strengths and guide them when trying to determine who is the best person for a team task. If space doesn't allow, type or have a teen volunteer type a summary sheet of the strengths people bring to the "party" and give teens copies to keep in their journals or notebooks.

Quote/End Quote

LEARNING CONCEPTS

- Qualities of leadership
- Inspiration and personal values
- Meaning of leadership
- Historical perspectives on leadership

(45–60 MINUTES)

This activity offers an interesting way for teens to explore and express their thoughts on leadership and being a leader. Participants work individually, first considering and interpreting quotes made by figures in history and then writing their own words of inspiration for leaders of the future. If used in a school setting, you can customize the activity to promote leadership across the curriculum by incorporating quotes from speakers or writers in various subject areas. If you wish, you can also frame the activity around broader topics such as character traits, service to others, or career exploration. Allow up to two 45-minute meetings if conducting the "Variation" or if teens want more time to work on their own personal quotes.

GOALS

Participants will:

- identify inspirational quotes related to leadership or being a leader
- interpret and apply quotes that represent leadership or being a leader
- clarify personal views and values related to leadership or being a leader

MATERIALS NEEDED

- Pen or pencil for each participant
- Sheet of paper or construction paper for each participant
- Handout: "Quotes" (page 103)
- *Optional*—Handout: Customizable "Quotes" form (page 104); markers, colored pencils, stickers, or other art supplies for decorating the "End Quote" sheets; various quotation books, collections, or Internet sites such as these (for "Variation"):

Bartlett's Familiar Quotations

The Oxford Dictionary of Quotations

www.bartleby.com (select "Respectfully Quoted" from drop-down menu)

www.online-literature.com/quotes/quotations.php

www.quotationspage.com

www.thinkexist.com

Make copies of the "Quotes" handout for each teen. If, instead, you will be selecting your own five quotes, use the customizable "Quotes" form (page 104), writing the quotes you have selected on one copy before making copies to distribute. Teens also will be writing their own words of inspiration, their own "End Quotes."

(If you will be conducting the variation where teens research quotes, make a copy of the customizable "Quotes" form on page 104 for each participant. Gather quotation books or collections of quotes and make them available for teens to access.)

Consider your own interpretations of the quotes you will hand out, and take time to write your own words of inspiration for future leaders on your own "End Quote" sheet so you will be prepared to share it during the group discussion. If teens will be decorating their "End Quotes," gather markers, colored pencils, and other supplies they will need.

Activity: Part 1

Pass out a copy of the "Quotes" handout to each teen. Explain the activity by saying:

This is a small collection of quotes related to the idea of leadership. Working on your own, read the first quote and write what it means to you in the space next to it. In your own words, explain how you think the quote applies to leadership or to being a leader. Then continue until you've considered and written about each quotation.

Allow 10 minutes for teens to read and write their interpretations. When everyone has finished, bring the group together and go through each quote, asking individuals to volunteer their interpretations. Depending on your group, this takes approximately 15–20 minutes.

After discussing the different interpretations, conduct the "Talk About It" questions for Part 1.

VARIATION

Instead of using the completed "Quotes" handout, pass out a copy of the blank "Quotes" handout to each teen. Allow 15–20 minutes for teens to use the resources you've provided to select and write down five quotes in the space indicated on the form. (If possible and if time permits, make copies of the individual worksheets so you can keep the quotes teens selected for use in future group discussions.) After teens have completed their handouts, have them pass their sheet to a different person in the group. Then explain the activity as described above and proceed with the rest of Part 1, having the students write what the quotes mean to them. If time is limited, you may want to use two meetings, one for

teens to look up and select their five quotes, the other for the interpretation and discussion process and for completing their own "End Quote" sheets.

Talk About It: Part 1

Take 10–15 minutes to have people share their interpretations of the quotes on the handout and discuss what they learned. Consider these discussion questions related to your group's experience:

- **What is it like to interpret and apply someone else's words about leadership to your own life?**
- **In what ways do the quotations illustrate how history has influenced views of leaders and leadership?**
- **What is a particularly inspirational quote that guides your life? What makes it inspirational to you?**

Activity: Part 2

Pass out blank sheets of paper and say:

You've considered what five people out of history had to say about leadership. What do *you* have to say? What words of inspiration would you like to offer future leaders? Write the following at the top of your sheet: "When others think of me, I want them to remember my very famous words of inspiration and insight. Here they are..." Think about it and write your own quote.

Allow a few minutes for teens to write their inspirational quotes. Take time to discuss Part 2 before closing

the meeting. If you are going to have participants illustrate or decorate their sheets, you may want to have them
do this on their own outside of group time or conduct this
part of the activity the next time the group meets.

Talk About It: Part 2

Take 5–10 minutes to share your own "End Quote" with
the group and invite teens to share theirs. As you share
and discuss the quotes, you might ask:

- **What does your quote mean to you?**
- **How do others interpret that quote?**

Wrapping Up

Display the completed "End Quote" sheets around the
room. If space doesn't allow, type or have a teen volunteer type a summary sheet of participants' quotes. Post a
copy of the complete collection and also make copies for
teens to keep in their journals or notebooks.

 Quotes

In the box next to each quote, write what the words mean to you.

Quote | Meaning

"I am not interested in picking up crumbs of compassion thrown from the table of someone who considers himself my master. I want the full menu of rights." —**Desmond Tutu**

Quote | Meaning

"All acts performed in the world begin in the imagination." —**Barbara Grizzuti Harrison**

Quote | Meaning

"In the beginner's mind there are many possibilities, but in the expert's mind there are few." —**Shunryu Suzuki**

Quote | Meaning

"Do not wait for leaders; do it alone, person to person." —**Mother Teresa of Calcutta**

Quote | Meaning

"Happiness always looks small while you hold it in your hands, but let it go, and you learn at once how big and precious it is." —**Maxim Gorky**

From *Teambuilding with Teens: Activities for Leadership, Decision Making, and Group Success* by Mariam G. MacGregor, M.S., copyright © 2008. Free Spirit Publishing Inc., Minneapolis, MN; www.freespirit.com. This page may be photocopied for individual, classroom, and group work only. For all other uses, call 800-735-7323.

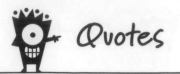 Quotes

In the boxes, write the five quotes you found. When you're finished, pass the sheet to someone else in the group who will write what the quotes mean to him or her:

Quote	Meaning

Quote	Meaning

Quote	Meaning

Quote	Meaning

Quote	Meaning

From *Teambuilding with Teens: Activities for Leadership, Decision Making, and Group Success* by Mariam G. MacGregor, M.S., copyright © 2008. Free Spirit Publishing Inc., Minneapolis, MN; www.freespirit.com. This page may be photocopied for individual, classroom, and group work only. For all other uses, call 800-735-7323.

Wise Sayings

- Qualities of leadership
- Inspiration and personal values
- Meaning of leadership
- Cultural perspectives on leadership

(35–45 MINUTES)

Proverbs and adages offer a springboard for teens to think about personal beliefs, character, and behavior. Because such statements are part of everyday conversations, most teens are familiar with learning lessons based on proverbs. Teens work in small groups to interpret proverbs, identifying the qualities of leadership they express and looking beyond the obvious to consider how the messages apply to their own lives and leadership experiences. You may also choose to focus the activity on broader topics the group is discussing, such as personal goal setting, service learning, or character development. If using the "Variation," allow 40–60 minutes for this activity.

GOALS

Participants will:

- identify proverbs and common sayings related to leadership or being a leader
- interpret and apply adages that represent leadership or being a leader
- clarify personal views and values related to leadership or being a leader

MATERIALS NEEDED

- Scissors
- Shoe box or other container
- Pen or pencil for each group of 3–5 teens
- Handouts: "Wise Sayings" (pages 109–110) and "Key to Wise Sayings" (page 113)
- *Optional*—Handout: Customizable "Wise Sayings" form (pages 111–112); various collections of proverbs from books or Web sites such as these (for "Variation"):

African Proverbs and Wisdom: A Collection for Every Day of the Year, from More Than Forty African Nations

The Oxford Dictionary of Proverbs

The Penguin Dictionary of Proverbs: Second Edition

The Prentice-Hall Encyclopedia of World Proverbs

Proverbs and Quotations from Nepal, Tibet, Asia, and the World

www.corsinet.com (choose "Brain Candy" and then choose "proverbs" under "quotations")

www.creativeproverbs.com

GETTING READY

If you wish, make a copy of the "Key to Wise Sayings" (page 113) for your own reference.

Make several copies of the "Wise Sayings" handout. Cut the sayings into slips, enough for each teen to have one slip. If you prefer providing your own selection of proverbs or sayings, use the customizable "Wise Sayings" form. Write the sayings on one copy before making additional copies and cutting the sayings into slips.

Place the slips in the shoe box or another small container. Teens will draw out slips; it is okay if more than one teen has the same saying.

(If you wish to use the "Variation" in which teens research proverbs, make a copy of the customizable "Wise Sayings" form for each participant. Gather collections of proverbs and make them available for teens to use. Internet access may be helpful.)

Determine how you will divide the large group into smaller groups of three to five people.

Setting the Stage

Using proverbs to talk about character and leadership is a fun and interesting way to give new meaning to phrases group members have heard throughout their lives.

Most teens can rattle off a list of proverbs, as long as they know what the term refers to. Proverbs are considered universal views that represent the truth in a concise way. Different people can say the same thing in different settings and most people can interpret what they mean. For example, authors use proverbs to set the tone for characters' behavior or actions; parents use proverbs to guide kids in making decisions; spiritual leaders use proverbs when guiding people in faith communities.

Proverbs are a little different from quotations, which are statements that can be attributed specifically to one person and which usually relate to an event or situation at a certain time in history. Many proverbs have sprung from a quote attributable to an individual, but most have become a part of language and expression without regard to who first made the statement. If you choose to write your own wise sayings for this activity, don't worry about the distinction between proverbs and quotations—use both if it's convenient.

When conducting the activity, you may want to ask teens to give you examples of proverbs they've heard before having them interpret the sayings on the handout. You'll also want to spend a little time exploring how proverbs guide daily behavior and what impact this behavior can have on the ways people are perceived by others.

If teen mentors are using this activity with younger kids, suggest that they use regular books children are reading, including early readers or picture books, to see if they can find proverbs in the context of the books. For this population, ask them to explain the "lesson" of the book, instead of asking for the proverb, giving examples of real proverbs so they understand what you want them to do.

The list of wise sayings for this activity are drawn from different cultures. The variety should help get teens really thinking and working together instead of quickly interpreting commonly known statements. In discussing the activities, you may want to refer to the general ideas about some of the qualities the proverbs represent ("Key to Wise Sayings," page 113). If you want to focus on adages that will be readily familiar to group members, use the form on pages 111–112 to make a customized list of "Wise Sayings."

Activity

Divide the large group into smaller groups of three to five participants. Have each group find a location where they can talk together without being distracted by other groups.

Take 2–3 minutes to discuss what proverbs are. Ask teens to explain this; if necessary, offer this definition: "Proverbs are short, well-known phrases or sentences that offer advice or state a general truth about life." You may want to share some simple examples ("When life gives you lemons, make lemonade," "When the going gets tough, the tough get going.") Invite teens to give examples as well. When it's clear that everyone understands the concept, explain the activity like this:

The slips of paper in this box all have a proverb on them. You'll each take one slip. Then, in your small groups, you'll work together to talk about what each

person's proverb means and to decide what qualities of leadership and human behavior the words express.

For example, suppose someone drew a slip that said, "The early bird catches the worm." What does that mean in terms of how people can behave? (Elicit ideas such as these: some people may be lazy, some may be eager, people who get going are more successful, and so forth.) **What does it mean for a group that wants to accomplish something? What could it mean for someone who is trying to be an effective leader? What qualities does this proverb suggest a leader might need?** (Examples might be initiative, quick thinking, or timeliness.)

Ask if anyone has questions. When you're sure everyone understands the task, say:

The slips of paper have space for you to write down the qualities. You don't need to write full sentences—it's fine to jot down words or thoughts.

Allow 10–15 minutes, depending on the size of the small groups, for teens to work together to evaluate the proverbs and write the qualities on each slip of paper. When all of the small groups have completed their slips, bring the group together and take another 15–20 minutes to go through the proverbs one by one, asking individuals to volunteer their group's interpretation of the saying. (Refer to the brief suggested qualities in the "Key to Wise Sayings" if this is helpful.)

VARIATION

Instead of using the completed "Wise Sayings" handout, pass out a copy of the blank "Wise Sayings" form to each group. Allow 5–10 minutes for teens to use the resources you've provided to select and write down one proverb for each member of the small group. (If possible and if time permits, make copies of individual teams' "Wise Sayings" sheets so you can keep the proverbs teens selected for use in future group discussions.) Then proceed with the rest of the activity as described above, allowing 10–15 minutes for the students to work in their small groups to identify the qualities of leadership and human behavior expressed by the proverb and another 15–20 minutes to share the proverbs with the larger group.

Talk About It

Take about 10 minutes to pull things together by discussing what teens learned from interpreting the proverbs. Consider questions like these related to your group's experience:

- **Do any of these statements best describe you as an individual? What statements seem to reflect your group?**

- **Are there statements you discussed that you think would be good guiding principles for the group? Explain.**

- **When you were working in your small groups, which proverbs were hard to figure out or interpret? Why? Which did most people relate to right away? Which turned out to be more complicated than they seemed at first? Explain.**

- **What is a particular proverb that guides your life? What makes it inspiring for you?**

- **How do you think everyday behavior for many people would change if they were often reminded of proverbs like these?**

Wrapping Up

Collect the slips and type or have a teen volunteer type a summary sheet of participants' proverbs and qualities. Post a copy of the complete collection and also make copies to give to teens at your next meeting.

Extending the Learning

This activity is rich in opportunities to extend the learning. Regardless of the ages of teens or kids taking part, proverbs, maxims, and other quick sayings resonate. There are several ways you can extend the activity:

Have teens read and discuss in small groups books such as *Writing from the Heart: Young People Share Their Wisdom* edited by Peggy Veljkovic and Arthur J. Schwartz (West Conshohocken, PA: Templeton Foundation Press, 2000) or *Teen Ink: What Matters* edited by Stephanie H. Meyer, John Meyer, and Peggy Veljkovic (Deerfield Beach, FL: HCI Teens, 2003).

Encourage teens to write essays focused on a proverb and to submit the essays to Teen Ink's "What Matters Contest." (Visit http://teenink.com and choose "Contests.") Or they can conduct a "Laws of Life" essay contest in their own community. You'll find details and guidelines at www.lawsoflife.org.

Start a "Wise Sayings" campaign. For learning that isn't associated with a book or national program, teens can coordinate their own "Wise Sayings" campaign around school or the community. Similar to the "Foundation for a Better Life" (www.values.com) billboard campaign seen in many communities, teens can design and display posters around school or the local area that remind people of simple phrases that make a big difference, using the list of proverbs from the "Wise Sayings" slips or creating a collection of their own.

Wise Sayings

What you give to others bears fruit for yourself. —**Senegalese proverb**

Qualities: _____

_____

A clear conscience is a soft pillow. —**German proverb**

Qualities: _____

_____

Words are like eggs: when they are hatched, they have wings. —**proverb from Madagascar**

Qualities: _____

_____

He who rides a tiger is afraid to dismount. —**Chinese proverb**

Qualities: _____

_____

It is better to conceal one's knowledge than to reveal one's ignorance. —**Spanish proverb**

Qualities: _____

_____

A promise is a cloud; fulfillment is rain. —**Saudi Arabian proverb**

Qualities: _____

_____

Life is a lamp flame; it needs a little oil now and then. —**Kashmiri proverb**

Qualities: _____

_____

Turn your face to the sun and the shadows fall behind you. —**proverb from New Zealand**

Qualities: _____

_____

From *Teambuilding with Teens: Activities for Leadership, Decision Making, and Group Success* by Mariam G. MacGregor, M.S., copyright © 2008. Free Spirit Publishing Inc., Minneapolis, MN; www.freespirit.com. This page may be photocopied for individual, classroom, and group work only. For all other uses, call 800-735-7323.

A lie travels round the world while truth is putting her boots on. —**French proverb**

Qualities: _____

_____

A man is not honest simply because he never had a chance to steal. —**Yiddish proverb**

Qualities: _____

_____

A society grows great when old men plant trees whose shade they know they shall never sit in. —**Greek proverb**

Qualities: _____

_____

A wise man makes his own decisions; an ignorant man follows the public opinion. —**Chinese proverb**

Qualities: _____

_____

Advice when most needed is least heeded. —**English proverb**

Qualities: _____

_____

Even a small thorn causes festering. —**Irish proverb**

Qualities: _____

_____

Everyone is kneaded out of the same dough but not baked in the same oven. —**Yiddish proverb**

Qualities: _____

_____

Life is a bridge. Cross over it, but build no house on it. —**Indian proverb**

Qualities: _____

_____

From *Teambuilding with Teens: Activities for Leadership, Decision Making, and Group Success* by Mariam G. MacGregor, M.S., copyright © 2008. Free Spirit Publishing Inc., Minneapolis, MN; www.freespirit.com. This page may be photocopied for individual, classroom, and group work only. For all other uses, call 800-735-7323.

Wise Sayings

Proverb: _____

Qualities: _____

_____

Proverb: _____

Qualities: _____

_____

Proverb: _____

Qualities: _____

_____

Proverb: _____

Qualities: _____

_____

Proverb: _____

Qualities: _____

_____

Proverb: _____

Qualities: _____

_____

Proverb: _____

Qualities: _____

_____

Proverb: _____

Qualities: _____

_____

MORE

From *Teambuilding with Teens: Activities for Leadership, Decision Making, and Group Success* by Mariam G. MacGregor, M.S., copyright © 2008. Free Spirit Publishing Inc., Minneapolis, MN; www.freespirit.com. This page may be photocopied for individual, classroom, and group work only. For all other uses, call 800-735-7323.

Proverb: _____

Qualities: _____

_____

Proverb: _____

Qualities: _____

_____

Proverb: _____

Qualities: _____

_____

Proverb: _____

Qualities: _____

_____

Proverb: _____

Qualities: _____

_____

Proverb: _____

Qualities: _____

_____

Proverb: _____

Qualities: _____

_____

Proverb: _____

Qualities: _____

_____

From *Teambuilding with Teens: Activities for Leadership, Decision Making, and Group Success* by Mariam G. MacGregor, M.S., copyright © 2008. Free Spirit Publishing Inc., Minneapolis, MN; www.freespirit.com. This page may be photocopied for individual, classroom, and group work only. For all other uses, call 800-735-7323.

Key to Wise Sayings

Here are some of the qualities expressed by the "Wise Sayings" on pages 109–110. You may want to add your own thoughts and ideas to this list, as well as other ideas teens come up with during the activity.

What you give to others bears fruit for yourself. —Senegalese Proverb
Qualities: empathy, treating others as one wants to be treated, acting ethically, kindness and generosity, thinking of others

A clear conscience is a soft pillow. —German proverb
Qualities: honesty, truthfulness, doing the right thing, integrity, acting ethically

Words are like eggs: when they are hatched, they have wings. —proverb from Madagascar
Qualities: thinking before speaking, freedom of expression, power of words, having one's voice heard

He who rides a tiger is afraid to dismount. —Chinese proverb
Qualities: willingness to confront meanness or violence, being real and true to oneself, modesty, humility

It is better to conceal one's knowledge than to reveal one's ignorance. —Spanish proverb
Qualities: modesty, thinking before speaking, empathy, understanding others, tolerance

A promise is a cloud; fulfillment is rain. —Saudi Arabian proverb
Qualities: commitment, follow-through, keeping one's word, inspiration, motivation, patience, trustworthiness, honor

Life is a lamp flame; it needs a little oil now and then. —Kashmiri proverb
Qualities: motivation, follow-through, hard work, reward and recognition, perseverance, life learning, personal growth

Turn your face to the sun and the shadows fall behind you. —proverb from New Zealand
Qualities: risk taking, not looking back, setting goals, overcoming obstacles, succeeding in spite of difficulties, being a leader, having followers, letting go, inspiration, looking toward the future, vision

A lie travels round the world while truth is putting her boots on. —French proverb
Qualities: keeping thoughts to oneself, thinking before speaking, truthfulness, understanding consequences, responsibility

A man is not honest simply because he never had a chance to steal. —Yiddish proverb
Qualities: personal standards, ethics, self-confidence, ability to stand up for beliefs, choosing to do the right thing, integrity

A society grows great when old men plant trees whose shade they know they shall never sit in. —Greek proverb
Qualities: vision, acting to benefit others, empathy, understanding consequences, altruism (doing good without expecting anything in return)

A wise man makes his own decisions; an ignorant man follows the public opinion. —Chinese proverb
Qualities: standing up for one's beliefs, confidence, open-mindedness, decision making, commitment, avoiding pitfalls of popularity

Advice when most needed is least heeded. —English proverb
Qualities: open-mindedness, overcoming stubbornness, listening to others, relying on others, problem solving

Even a small thorn causes festering. —Irish proverb
Qualities: dealing with problems instead of avoiding them, not blowing things out of proportion, being realistic

Everyone is kneaded out of the same dough but not baked in the same oven. —Yiddish proverb
Qualities: tolerance, diversity, open-mindedness, inclusive of others, self-confidence

Life is a bridge. Cross over it, but build no house on it. —Indian proverb
Qualities: vision, resourcefulness, not taking advantage of others, understanding consequences, motivation, willingness to change and move forward

From *Teambuilding with Teens: Activities for Leadership, Decision Making, and Group Success* by Mariam G. MacGregor, M.S., copyright © 2008. Free Spirit Publishing Inc., Minneapolis, MN; www.freespirit.com. This page may be photocopied for individual, classroom, and group work only. For all other uses, call 800-735-7323.

Social Issues

Power Trip

Fruit Salad

Inside Out

Choosing Sides

Peace and Violence Webs

Power Trip

┌─────────────────────────────────────┐
│ **LEARNING CONCEPTS**   │
│   │
│ • Understanding power   • Making a difference │
│ • Understanding the need for empathy and tolerance │
└─────────────────────────────────────┘

(45 MINUTES)

This activity, while uncomfortable for some, serves as a catalyst for discussing the meaning and uses of power and guides teens toward understanding their roles in everyday interactions and social change. As three teams of teens, each with a different level of power, try to solve a problem assigned to them, it becomes clear that more power naturally falls to teams with greater resources. Nonetheless, with guidance from the facilitator and insight from participants, even the team with the most limited resources can have the greatest influence on the final outcome. You may want to use this activity prior to embarking on a service project or mission trip.

GOALS

Participants will:

- gain a basic understanding of the influence power can have in group settings
- recognize how individuals and groups can make a difference
- increase personal awareness of the need for empathy and tolerance toward others

MATERIALS NEEDED

- Cardstock or other stiff paper
- Safety pins, one per group member
- Handouts: "Power Trip Rules" (page 118) and "Power Trip Team Tasks" (page 119)
- *Optional*—Newsprint, marker, masking tape

GETTING READY

Using the cardstock, cut out an even number of circles, triangles, and squares, making sure you have as many shapes as there are teens in the group.

Make three copies of the "Power Trip Rules" and "Power Trip Team Tasks" handouts, one for each team. For the rules handout, fill in the name of the community all three teams belong to (your youth group, school, organization, city, or club) in the blank on each sheet. For the tasks handout, write in one goal for all three teams to work toward. (Examples: plan the prom, plan a service project, conduct a teen leader election, plan a mission, address a school safety issue, deal with drug or alcohol problems, plan an annual carnival.) The goal you identify should be real and relevant enough that participants will readily immerse themselves in problem solving to accomplish a particular outcome.

If possible, copy the "Power Trip Rules" and the "Power Trip Team Tasks" by hand onto newsprint and hang them where teens will be able to see them. Fold the bottom half up over the top half of each sheet (tape it gently to hold it) so the information remains covered until the activity begins.

Organize the space in which you will conduct the activity so there are three distinct areas identified as the Circle Area, the Triangle Area, and the Square Area, and post a labeled shape in each area to designate it. The Circle Area should be larger than the other two, with comfortable chairs or desks for all team members. The Triangle Area should be slightly smaller, with a few chairs or desks, but not enough for everyone on the team. The Square Area should be the smallest space and have only one or two chairs.

Review the rules and tasks on the handouts and then determine how you will divide the group into three smaller teams; see "Setting the Stage" for guidance. You may want to jot down group assignments prior to the meeting.

Setting the Stage

Addressing the role of power in modern society can be challenging, but learning the positive and negative impacts of power is important for young people. At an early age, children become aware of the role power plays in their lives. They experience this in many ways: when authority figures direct what they do or when peers divide into cliques. The skew of power in this activity illustrates how it is arbitrarily distributed in real life. Teens have no choice about what team they belong to, so you're able to address how power can be given or taken away at any time. It's an excellent opportunity for participants to recognize how they can perpetuate a negative use of power or make decisions that expand power to all groups.

The activity set-up is unfair from the beginning: Circles have the most established power, Squares the least. Each team has a different budget, different options for working across teams, and even a different environment (in terms of space and comfort) to work in. But it doesn't need to remain out of balance. If teens are struggling because their team is at a disadvantage, remind them that they have their voices and ingenuity to rely on. Encourage frustrated teens to think beyond the written rules to identify ways they can plan and get their ideas across. For example, if Circles are being domineering early in the activity, Triangles or Squares can choose how to react. They might remain silent or gather in one small part of their zone and shut out the Circles. They might make use of the times Circles come to their area to negotiate for things ("We're happy to help with your request if you'll agree to work with us on ours").

Teens who are used to having little power often tend to be the ones to take the greatest liberty with the power they're given. Some participants may seem to forget how it feels to be an underdog or to be taken advantage of by others. Over time, though, obvious power can give way to perceived power, leading to a changed sense—or an actual change in distribution—of that power.

How you divide the teams has a significant impact on how the activity plays out. Regardless of whether teens are used to having power, they may struggle as members of any team. You'll want each team to contain a true mix of teens with diverse attitudes and expectations of power, voice, and influence. This may mean assigning less vocal students to be Circles or Triangles and the most vocal or dominating to be Squares. Consider placing teens with informal influence on different teams from teens with formal leadership roles. Split up close friends.

How the activity unfolds will differ from group to group due to setting, diversity, group rapport, and other independent factors. Sometimes tension runs high. For example, some Circles may want to use their power with a heavy hand, while some Triangles and Squares may underestimate how difficult it can be to get things done unless power is used effectively and efficiently. In some cases, the activity tends to progress with less tension—Circles may quickly decide to include everyone in the process, bringing all three teams together and giving everyone an equal voice and role in accomplishing the goal. But even the "nicest" groups can be diverted by the original set-up of the activity, with Circles trying to maintain their power and control over the other groups. You'll want to be prepared for a variety of responses from teens and ready to offer suggestions, encouragement, or redirection as needed.

Activity

Give teens a circle, square, or triangle along with a safety pin and ask them to secure it to the front of their shirt. Show them where they are to gather with others on their team. Next explain the activity like this:

> **Today you will do a role play called "Power Trip." In the role play, you will work in teams to solve a problem together. Let's get started.**
> **Welcome to _____.** (Name the community you've written on the rules handout.) **Even though you're in three different teams, you all have a common goal for this meeting: _____.** (State the goal you've written on the tasks handout.) **Before you get started, there are a few ground rules that I'll explain. Then you will have a couple of minutes to ask me questions. Once any team starts strategizing, I'll start keeping time. You'll have 25 minutes to work toward the overall goal.**

Pass out the "Power Trip Team Tasks" handout to each team; if you have displayed the tasks on a chart, uncover the chart. Read through the tasks with the group. Then pass out the "Power Trip Rules," reveal the chart if you've posted one, and read through the rules. Allow a few minutes for any questions. If teens say that it's unfair, you can respond matter-of-factly:

> **This is the activity. Please follow the guidelines and roles as indicated on your team's handout. We'll talk about it when you're done.**

Walk around the room to maintain order and to provide subtle ideas or encouragement for teams that seem stuck. Once time is up, ask teens to take a seat where they are. Depending on how the activity progressed for your group, take a few minutes to let teens blow off steam and get out of their team roles. Then use the remaining time to conduct the "Talk About It" discussion.

Talk About It

Consider these discussion questions related to this activity:

- **What went through your mind as you read through the rules and tasks? Let's hear from some Circles, Triangles, and Squares.**
- **Circles, how did your team start working together? Was that how you were working at the end? Triangles, how did your team work together from beginning to end? Squares?**
- **The rules set up the power distribution at the beginning of the activity. Did the distribution of power change? In what way? How? Was there a turning point? Did individuals influence the rest of the teams? If so, what happened? If not, why not?**
- **What happens in everyday life if all the power is with one group? Does this type of system exist in the real world? Can it be changed? Explain.**
- **Do you think individuals can make a difference in changing who has power, how it gets used, and how decisions get made? Explain.**

Wrapping Up

If time allows, have teens brainstorm how they'd change the division of power in the activity based on what they know after experiencing it. If possible, have them identify ways they can confront "power trips" in real life and commit to taking small steps toward doing this as a team.

Extending the Learning

Hold a follow-up discussion. It may be necessary and useful to revisit the activity the next time your group meets, so consider allotting 15–20 minutes at your next gathering for any follow-up comments or discussion.

Connect to the group's actual project. If you do this activity prior to a service project or mission trip, apply the lessons to the specific task the group will be undertaking. After the project or mission is completed, discuss what was learned and how teens approached the project differently based on their "Power Trip" experience of having or lacking power.

Try a simulated experience. For more mature groups capable of abstracting the lessons of this activity, conduct StarPower, a real-time, face-to-face, non–computer-based simulation addressing power and social movement. It takes several hours and is best used with older teens. (The product is available from Simulation Training Systems, 1-800-942-2900, www.simulationtrainingsystems.com.)

Power Trip Rules

1. Everyone will be a member of one of three teams: Circles, Triangles, or Squares. All are members of _____.

2. The Circles will occupy the Circle Area and possess $7,000 of the $10,000 budget.

3. The Triangles will occupy the Triangle Area and possess the remaining $3,000 of the budget.

4. The Squares will occupy the Square Area.

5. Circles are free to use any of the three areas they wish. They may communicate at any time with Squares and Triangles.

6. Triangles are free to use the Square Area as well as their own. They may communicate at any time with Squares. If they wish to communicate with Circles, they may request the Circles' permission to do so.

7. Squares are free to use their own area. If they wish to communicate with Triangles, they may request the Triangles' permission to do so. Squares are not allowed to contact Circles in any way unless they've been invited to do so by the Circles.

8. Circles are free to make any changes in the rules they wish. Such decisions take effect immediately and do not need to be voted on or approved by Triangles or Squares.

From *Teambuilding with Teens: Activities for Leadership, Decision Making, and Group Success* by Mariam G. MacGregor, M.S., copyright © 2008. Free Spirit Publishing Inc., Minneapolis, MN; www.freespirit.com. This page may be photocopied for individual, classroom, and group work only. For all other uses, call 800-735-7323.

 Power Trip Team Tasks

The goal is to _____.

 1. Circles have overall responsibility for making sure everyone works toward this goal and for using resources effectively. They may use their money in any way they believe will contribute to achieving this goal. If they see flaws in the way the system is organized, they can redesign it to improve it.

 2. Triangles are responsible for the effective use of the money they've received and for working toward the goal. They should help the Circles identify any problems with how the system is organized and help Circles find solutions to any problems that could affect achieving the goal.

3. Squares are to use their resources as effectively as possible to help achieve the goal.

From *Teambuilding with Teens: Activities for Leadership, Decision Making, and Group Success* by Mariam G. MacGregor, M.S., copyright © 2008. Free Spirit Publishing Inc., Minneapolis, MN; www.freespirit.com. This page may be photocopied for individual, classroom, and group work only. For all other uses, call 800-735-7323.

Fruit Salad

- Understanding and overcoming stereotypes
- Recognizing different points of view • Valuing individuality

(35–45 MINUTES)

From a selection of similar fruits each teen selects one piece. Individually, they get to know their fruit's distinguishing qualities before returning it to the large pile where the fruits are thoroughly mixed up. Then participants are asked to retrieve their piece and explain its unique properties to others in the group. The overall goal is to increase awareness of stereotyping and show how individuality is overlooked when stereotypes are preserved. The activity's light approach to a serious topic allows teens to feel comfortable talking about prejudice and considering different points of views. Discussion revolves around overcoming group judgments, finding ways to identify what makes people unique, and determining how stereotyping can be avoided.

GOALS

Participants will:

- gain a basic understanding of what it means to accept and value individuality
- learn about the role individuals, group members, and leaders have in overcoming stereotypes
- clarify personal beliefs on challenging topics and be able to express their opinions

MATERIALS NEEDED

- Pieces of one type of fruit (such as all lemons, all limes, or all apples), one piece per participant
- Sheet of writing paper for each participant
- Pens or pencils, one for each teen
- Chalkboard and chalk, or whiteboard or flip chart and marker
- *Optional*—Large collection of unique buttons, many more than the number of participants, stored in a clear box, plastic shoe box, or similar container (see "Variation")

GETTING READY

Purchase enough of one kind of fruit so that each teen can have his or her own piece. Select a type that will withstand frequent handling without resulting in obvious change of color or texture. Choose individual pieces of fruit that look similar when in a group yet have unique characteristics when held alone.

Have writing paper and pens or pencils available for participants. Organize chairs in a circle around a central table where the fruit will be placed.

Setting the Stage

Time is spent in the activity defining and discussing stereotypes. This discussion takes place *after* teens have evaluated the pile of fruit and become directly attached to their own piece. If you conduct such a discussion prior to the activity, the nature of the activity changes, and teens are less likely to move from the broad to the concrete in applying the learning concepts. Focusing teens on something tactile, like fruit, helps make the topic of stereotypes and individuality real and helps keep the discussion from becoming about "us" and "them." Because teens become attached to their items, they're less likely to push the responsibility for confronting stereotypes off to others, and will have a greater sense of their role in changing their own stereotyping behavior.

There are many ways to address stereotypes. Establishing a common understanding of the topic, as well as learning ways to overcome stereotyping, is a lifelong process. Younger kids aren't always as aware as older ones of their tendency to stereotype. Teens tend to understand stereotyping best as it applies to cliques, group affiliations (positive and negative), and other adolescent relationships.

Teens in groups that are relatively homogeneous racially, culturally, or socio-economically may have a harder time recognizing the impact of stereotyping. It can be helpful to identify other less obvious but still distinctive characteristics, behaviors, or outlooks that distinguish people from one another. Depending on your group, you might cite examples such as gender, sexual orientation, hobbies, interests, daily routines, attitudes about specific social activities, religious or political beliefs, and so on. When teens from homogeneous groups are exposed to cultural and ethnic differences through experiential learning and discussion, they enhance their ability to transfer what is learned to their future experiences (moving to a new community, participating in a cultural festival, playing sports against a team from a different area, attending college, and so forth).

If, during the activity, teens are unable to identify their own piece of fruit, you'll want to be prepared to address, in a nonjudgmental way, why it is difficult for them to do so. This can lead to an excellent discussion about how people sometimes lump everyone of a certain culture or race into the same group (for example, stating that all girls or women are overly emotional, that all males are aggressive, or that all white/black/Asian people look the same) and how ignorance can occur even when people don't intend it to. Part of this discussion can address the difference between having no experience recognizing individual characteristics and choosing to remain ignorant and to demean certain groups.

You can frame the discussion more specifically around the role leaders have in overcoming stereotypes with questions such as: "Why should leaders be expected to confront stereotypes?" "What can happen to a team if a leader acts in ways that perpetuate stereotypes?" "In what ways can leaders be role models to change perceived stereotypes about others?"

The nature of this activity makes it ideal to use with young kids as well. The younger the population, the more concrete the discussion, so you will need to be prepared with clear examples and suggestions for how kids can apply what they've learned.

Activity

Place the fruit on a desk or table in the center of the room. Allow teens to sit wherever they'd like in the circle, as long as they can see the pile of fruit. Introduce the activity by saying:

Today we are going to get to know some fruit. (Expect and allow for giggles.) **In front of you is a pile of fruit. Tell me what you see.**

Allow 2–3 minutes for teens to give you their immediate impression of the pile of fruit. Their responses will most likely be about the pile as a whole, and not about a specific piece of fruit. Following this, ask teens to come to the pile, select an individual piece of fruit, and return to their seat. This will take up to 5 minutes. Pass out paper and pens or pencils and then explain:

You're to get to know the piece of fruit you've picked. I want you to look at it carefully and get very familiar with it. Look at its skin, smell it, feel it, and think of how to describe it. During the next 5–10 minutes, give your fruit a name and write down at least three specific qualities about your fruit.

Allow teens time to evaluate their fruit. While they're doing this, walk around the room to encourage or support them as they are thinking of things to write about their piece of fruit.

When time is up, have everyone place their piece of fruit back in the pile and sit down again. Mix the pile up. Ask teens to return to the fruit pile, find their original piece of fruit, and take it back to their chair and sit down. Then, taking turns, have each teen introduce his or her fruit to the group, tell the fruit's name, and read the list of qualities that describe the fruit. Ask each participant:

When you went back to find your fruit in the pile, how did you know it was your piece?

After everyone has introduced and explained their piece of fruit, guide a 5- to 10-minute lesson on stereotypes. Being by asking:

Who can tell me what stereotyping is?

Allow responses, writing them on the chalkboard or newsprint to summarize their responses. Then continue:

Stereotyping is when people prejudge a group of people. It is when they don't see an individual in any way except as a member of a certain group. How does the fruit activity you just did highlight how quickly and easily stereotyping can occur? What else did you learn from the activity?

Invite responses. Teens typically explain that at first they just saw a pile of fruit, but after getting to know an individual piece, the pile looked different. If not, guide them to this understanding. Finish the lesson by asking:

What are some common stereotypes you have heard? Have you ever been the object of stereotyping? Give some examples.

Write the common stereotypes and examples on the board or flip chart. Leave what you've written visible as you move on to the "Talk About It" discussion.

VARIATION

Set up the room in the same way, but instead of putting fruit on the center table, place a box or bowl filled with buttons on it. It is important that your collection be made up of many colors and designs; make sure it includes unique buttons as well as some that look similar but still have distinctive markings. Collections of used buttons are easy to find at large discount stores, at hobby and craft stores, and on the Internet.

When it comes to having teens choose an individual button, ask them to select one that really attracts them. Then conduct the activity as described. During discussions, your questions will refer to the buttons they selected rather than fruit.

Talk About It

Allow teens to keep their piece of fruit. Then take 10–15 minutes to discuss questions like these related to this activity:

- **How did your opinion of the pile of fruit change from when you walked into the room until you finished retrieving your fruit the second time? Why did you feel differently once you "knew" an individual piece of fruit from the pile?**

- **How often do you jump to conclusions about a group of people the first time you see them? How does it feel to be one of the members of a group where people jump to conclusions about you?**

- **In a group where people have different views, how can you prevent the group from being insensitive to some views or ideas? What if you have members who don't care what others think and want their views to drive what the group does?**

- **As individuals, what steps can people take to eliminate stereotyping? What about as a group?**

- **How can individuals challenge others when they stereotype groups or individuals? What do you think leaders need to do to confront stereotyping? What can a group do if a leader is stereotyping groups or individuals?**

Wrapping Up

Allow teens to keep their piece of fruit (or they can trade it with others as a symbolic gesture of committing to challenge stereotypes). Encourage them to put their descriptive papers in their notebooks or journals. Suggest they write some thoughts about ways they've been stereotyped and how they've stereotyped others and the steps they'll take to confront damaging stereotypes when they see or hear them.

Extending the Learning

In this book, you may want to conduct the preceding activity, "Power Trip" (pages 115–119), which addresses the impact power has on groups, particularly because preserving stereotypes often has something to do with one group's efforts to maintain power over other groups.

Delve deeper. Correlate this activity with topics such as the Holocaust or other genocides such as those that are occurring or have occurred in the Sudan, Armenia, and Bosnia to provide a real-life look at how stereotypes can lead to dramatic individual and group behaviors.

Visit one of the many Web sites that provide lesson plans or resources for further exploration of stereotypes and their impact. These sites include teen resources as well as resources for elementary-age students, which can be useful for teens working as mentors with a younger population:

The Anti-Defamation League (www.adl.org)

Although the emphasis is on anti-Semitism, the Web site has contemporary essays, public policy information, and historical resources addressing a wide range of topics including stereotyping, bias, prejudice, extremism, and securing justice and fair treatment for all.

Teaching Tolerance (www.tolerance.org)

This organization offers a free quarterly magazine, resources, and lesson plans based on real ways schools and communities address bias, stereotypes, and prejudice and promote tolerance around the world. The lesson plans are well researched and engaging.

Media Awareness Network (MNet) (www.media-awareness.ca)

MNet is a Canadian nonprofit dedicated to developing media literacy programs for kids and teens. The organization produces online programs and resources, relevant to worldwide audiences, that teach young people how to "read" the messages they see on TV, the Internet, and other entertainment outlets. Select "For Teachers" to access lesson plans; search the lesson plan menu by highlighting "stereotyping," "gender portrayal," or "diversity portrayal." This site also includes ideas for educating kids and teens on how groups are portrayed in stereotypical ways. Resources are arranged by age and developmental appropriateness.

Family Education (www.familyeducation.com/home)
Teacher Vision (www.teachervision.fen.com)

These two sites are affiliated with educational curriculum developers and publishers that offer resources, lesson plans, and age-appropriate scripts for talking and learning about stereotypes. Type "stereotypes" in the search box for either site to get to the information needed. The Family Education site has more in terms of talking openly with children about stereotypes and prejudice, which could be used by teen mentors to increase comfort with discussing difficult topics with younger kids.

Inside Out

LEARNING CONCEPTS

- Dealing with cliques • Dealing with exclusion
- Including and accepting others

(30–35 MINUTES)

Teens are unknowingly experts at excluding others from their groups. The exclusion isn't always deliberate and this activity reinforces how simple actions can make a huge impact on the people being excluded. Participants role-play scenarios in which they first exclude, then partially include, and finally fully include an "outsider." Throughout the activity, the group learns to recognize how they contribute to or detract from an atmosphere that is accepting of others. They are encouraged to explore how they treat others they perceive to be outsiders—whether in relation to their sports team, club, youth group, or group of friends—and to evaluate what they can do when other group members are determined to exclude people from decisions or projects. If your group struggles with cliques, the activity provides an effective and sensitive way to bring real-life attitudes and behaviors into focus. With younger kids, this is a good activity for addressing bullying, especially girl-to-girl bullying behaviors. You will need chairs that can be placed together tightly in a circle.

GOALS

Participants will:

- identify attitudes that make others feel excluded from a group
- learn more about personal behaviors that may make others feel bullied or put down
- discuss ways to be more accepting of others outside a group

MATERIALS NEEDED

- Several business-size envelopes
- Handout: "Inside-Out Role Plays" (page 127)

GETTING READY

If your group is small, you can have everyone participate in one group of up to 10–12 teens. With a larger group, you'll want to create smaller groups of 6–10 students who will do the activity simultaneously. Strive to have each group include a diverse set of teens; avoid having existing friends end up in one group. You may want to determine how you'll divide your group prior to the meeting.

Make a copy of the "Inside-Out Role Plays" handout for each group. Fold them and place each one in an envelope.

Organize the chairs into close circles, each with enough chairs for all but one member of each group.

If possible, have extra chairs available somewhere in the room.

Read the "Inside-Out Role Plays" so you fully understand the three scenarios the groups will enact.

Setting the Stage

Reflecting on exclusionary attitudes and behaviors can be difficult for teens, who don't want to be perceived as people who discourage others from joining their groups. Often, the students who are excluded the most in daily life quickly recognize the emotions and attitudes taking place in this activity. Teens who exclude others in real life, or who are members of cliques known for being exclusive, often don't make a personal connection right away. If this occurs in your group, it's important to address it during the activity.

You will be asking for a volunteer from each group to play the role of an "outsider." It is tempting to call on individuals who often exclude others to serve as these "outsiders." This can be effective, but it can also backfire. On the one hand, volunteers may have their eyes opened because they are able to experience empathy. On the other hand, teens may become aggressive and overly mean toward such a volunteer. If this happens, it can lead to a situation in which the volunteer shuts down and refuses to see any connection to real-life behavior.

Also, some teens appear exclusionary when in fact they are extremely shy. If a shy teen were to take the "outsider" role, the activity could backfire by causing the person to feel so exposed that she or he would be unable to engage in the role playing. In general, it is best to select a volunteer who can withstand being the object of both negative and positive attitudes.

The best way to address individual behavior that comes up in the activity is to incorporate this during the "Talk About It" segment.

Activity

There are three scenarios to role-play in this activity; each one has the larger group relate to the individual they are excluding in a different way. Conduct all three scenarios *before* discussing what occurred during any of the role playing.

Divide participants into the small groups you established. Open the activity by saying:

Each group is going to role-play three different situations that deal with how people are included in, or excluded from, your group. In order to do this, choose a volunteer from your group who'll play the role of "outsider" for the activity. This needs to be someone who can deal with being *excluded*—left out or ignored—*and included*. Your volunteer also needs to be comfortable with the rest of you playing parts where you may say some rude or unkind things toward him or her as part of the role play. People may be saying some things that aren't true but could hurt a person's feelings in real life.

Allow 2–3 minutes for each group to select their volunteer. (While it's unlikely that a group will have a hard time picking a volunteer or that you'll be concerned about the selection a group makes, you might suggest a certain person to play the "outsider.") Ask those volunteers to step out of the room for a few minutes where they can't hear the instructions being given to the remaining teens. Tell the groups:

In your small groups, you're going to role-play that you are a group of friends. I'll give you written instructions for role-playing three different situations. The situations are called *scenarios*. Do not share these with the volunteers when they return. When the volunteers come back in the room, I will give them spoken instructions to become part of your groups. Then you will begin with Scenario A. You can do what you need to do to make the outsiders feel excluded, but don't go overboard. Avoid raising your voices and do not touch one another or say mean, personal things that could be taken for real. I'll let you know when it's time to move to Scenario B and when it's time to move on to Scenario C.

Give each group an envelope and allow a few minutes for the groups to look at the instructions and ask questions before inviting the volunteers back into the room. Have them stand near the group that they started with and explain their role:

You're going to play "outsiders" to your group. The groups have been given different situations to role-play, and they may or may not let you become part of their group. They will not share the instructions they've been given with you. You can do whatever it takes to become part of the group except push, shove, or use other physical force. Also, avoid raising your voice, but feel free to use discussion, persuasion, or negotiation to get in. Any questions?

Allow a few minutes for questions and then indicate that the groups are to begin with Scenario A. After 3–5 minutes of role-playing, announce that the group should move on to Scenario B. Once more, after 3–5 minutes of role-playing Scenario B, announce that the group should move on to Scenario C. Allow the activity to end after groups have role-played Scenario C for 5 minutes.

With the groups remaining in their circles, begin the "Talk About It" discussion.

Talk About It

Scenario C leaves the groups with a friendly rapport, but the "outsiders" usually remember what it's like to be excluded. In addition to connecting the experience to real-life situations, consider these discussion questions:

- How many of you could relate to what happened in this activity? How many of you have been the person excluded from a group? What was it like? How did you deal with it?

- For those of you who were "outsiders" in the role plays, how did each situation feel? If this were real life, how would you begin to feel or think about yourself and about others?

- For those of you in the groups, what did it feel like to exclude someone? Do you think people always know when they're excluding others? Explain. If you see people excluding others, how can you bring the behavior to their attention?

- Be honest, and raise your hands if you think you exclude others from your real-life groups. Can anyone volunteer to share why you think you do this? Do you think your behavior will change after today?

- In real life, what happens when people pretend to accept someone into their group but ignore or put down the person? What might happen if a person is constantly rejected or excluded?

- Is it possible that people who bully others were at one time excluded from a group? Explain.

- What can you use from this activity to help you focus on being more inclusive—more welcoming—toward others in everyday life?

Wrapping Up

When the activity is finished, you might consider bringing teens together to share what they appreciate about being part of the group and acknowledging others in an inclusive way. Ask teens to spend the next few days observing different situations where they see people being excluded (or find themselves excluding others) and to write their thoughts in their journals or notebooks. Encourage them to write about ways they can change their behavior if they're excluding others or if they witness exclusion but don't feel comfortable confronting it.

 Inside-Out Role Plays

Scenario A

In this situation, your circle of friends will keep your backs to the "outsider" and completely exclude him or her from your group. When that person tries to join your group, move closer to each other or give the person a disapproving look. You can say things that are rude, but do *not* say hurtful things that could be misunderstood to seem like you really mean them. Here are examples of what you might say:

• "Isn't it annoying when people don't get the hint that they aren't welcome?"

• "Maybe we should meet somewhere else where people can't butt in."

• "I wish we could just choose who'll be members of this group and not worry about others trying to join us."

Scenario B

When the time comes to move into Scenario B, you can say something like: "Oh, hi, ___(person's name). I didn't see you there. Come join us!"

In this situation, your circle of friends will let the outsider into your group. You can do this by making room in your circle and sharing a chair or by bringing another chair into the group for the person. Once you've invited the "outsider" in, though, ignore the person. Speak to one another and to anyone *except* the "outsider." Barely pay attention to the new person and change the topic if the "outsider" says anything or tries to join the conversation.

Scenario C

When the time comes to move into Scenario C, you can say something like, "Hey, ___(name of person)__, you've been trying to share your ideas this whole time. We'd love to hear what you think."

In this situation, your circle of friends will truly include the "outsider" and try to make the person feel welcome. You are to invite him or her into your conversation, asking questions and inviting ideas from that person. Respond sincerely to the person's comments. If you want, you can apologize for excluding the person and explain that you didn't realize how much you have in common.

From *Teambuilding with Teens: Activities for Leadership, Decision Making, and Group Success* by Mariam G. MacGregor, M.S., copyright © 2008. Free Spirit Publishing Inc., Minneapolis, MN; www.freespirit.com. This page may be photocopied for individual, classroom, and group work only. For all other uses, call 800-735-7323.

Choosing Sides

- Self-awareness • Respecting different points of view
- Personal values • Understanding social issues

(25–45 MINUTES)

As you read from a list of statements, teens choose a side of the room to stand on indicating that they agree or disagree with each statement. They can also choose to stand on a line in the middle of the room, showing that they aren't sure or that their answer depends on the situation. Then participants are asked to explain why they have made their particular choice. This activity lends itself to rich discussions about respecting and understanding different viewpoints. You can use the statements provided, modify them, or write your own. You will need ample space for everyone to move freely.

GOALS

Participants will:

- gain a basic understanding of other points of view
- learn about the values group members hold regarding different social issues
- clarify personal beliefs about challenging topics and be able to express their opinions

MATERIALS NEEDED

- Masking tape
- 2 sheets of paper, 8½" x 11"
- Marker
- Handout: "Statements for Choosing Sides" (page 131)

GETTING READY

Make a copy of the "Statements for Choosing Sides" handout for your own use.

Move any tables, chairs, or desks out of the way to create an open area for movement.

Lay a piece of masking tape across the middle of the floor to divide the room into sides. Write "Agree" and "Yes" on one sheet of paper, and "Disagree" and "No" on another. Tape the sheets on the opposite walls.

ACCOMMODATIONS

For groups where teens have physical challenges requiring crutches or a wheelchair, this activity can still be conducted as described; it may require a larger space for movement.

Setting the Stage

The handout provides a list of sample statements. Choose statements that work best for your group and time limit. You may want to modify or add to the list of statements. While it's important to select statements that suit the population of the group, be certain that the ideas will challenge participants to think about tough issues, take a stand, and move beyond their comfort zones. Over time, you can compile statements from different groups you work with to add to your collection.

Prior to conducting the activity, establish or reaffirm group norms for maintaining open and productive communication around controversial topics. Explain that the purpose of the activity is to think about their own position on a topic and to be open-minded about other people's perspectives. The goal isn't to have teens convince each other to change their opinions or beliefs. Still, some of the statements may lead to loudly voiced opinions, so to reinforce respect for individual views and to keep the activity moving forward, be prepared to moderate one-to-one discussion while allowing all voices to be heard. (See "Dealing with Difficult Discussions," page 5, for more on maintaining a respectful group environment.) If necessary, remind teens that when they're asked to share an opinion, it's just that—an opinion—and that all opinions are equally valuable and worthy of respect. If there is too much in-depth conversation or arguing, you won't get through many statements and some teens may feel that their views have been dismissed. An atmosphere of conflict will also make some teens check out from the activity.

Moving to a side of the room encourages participants to think about and commit to personal beliefs. By physically "taking a stand," teens actively illustrate their values and choices while thinking through how to explain them. Seeing how and where people move with each statement reminds the group that people can share some beliefs, yet not others, and that they may express them similarly or differently. There may be some surprises when teens move to a side that others aren't expecting. When this occurs, take time *at that point* to talk about people's reactions instead of waiting until the activity's end. For example, you might say, "You seem surprised that Kayla agrees. Why did you expect her to make a different choice?" At the same time, be careful not to put people on the spot; allow them the freedom to say as much or as little as they're comfortable with.

Activity

Ask teens to gather on one side of the room. Explain the activity like this:

> **As you can see, the room is set up with two different sides. I am going to read a series of statements. You'll make a choice that reflects your opinion or belief about each statement. If you agree with a statement or would answer yes to it, you'll move to one side. If you disagree or would answer no, you'll move to the other. The taped line down the middle of the floor represents a choice of "I don't know" or "It depends on the situation." How you feel about some statements may be very clear to you. With others, you may struggle to decide where you stand. If you really can't choose, you may go to the middle, but try to make firm choices about the statements. No matter what, you need to move to the location that shows your opinion about the statement; you can't just remain in one spot the entire time.**
>
> **After I've read a statement and everyone has moved, I'll invite you to explain why you're standing where you are. This is an opportunity for everyone to explain their choices. It's not a time to judge each other or to argue or try to persuade people to see things your way. As you listen to what others say, your goal is to be open-minded and respectful about different points of view.**

Briefly answer any questions, and then begin. One by one, read the statements, allowing time for teens to move to their chosen spots and inviting volunteers to explain why they made the choice they did. Allot 20–25 minutes to read as many statements as appropriate based on how your group is responding and on the dynamics of the process.

After reading the list of statements, ask teens to take a seat and conduct the "Talk About It" discussion.

VARIATION

Instead of selecting from the list of statements included, ask every participant to bring or email you ahead of time a statement, related to a current social issue, that peers can agree or disagree with. You may give them an example from the list so they have a sense of the types of statements you're looking for. Prior to conducting the activity, have teens hand in their statements so you can organize them. Set up the room and conduct the activity in the same way.

Talk About It

Talking about this activity can take 10–15 minutes. As part of your discussion, you may want to explore what it was like to discuss personal beliefs without arguing with others to change their point of view. Depending on what the group says, you can lead a discussion about how the group shows tolerance toward the ideas and values of members when it's obvious that individuals believe different things. You may also want to discuss what shared values the group holds. Consider these other discussion questions related to the activity:

- **What statements really made you think? Explain.**

- **Are there situations where your friends or family expect you to act or believe a certain way even though you don't? Explain. Did any of these confusing feelings or thoughts arise during this activity?**

- **Have you ever been in a situation where you were *unable* to let your true feelings show? What did you do? If you've never experienced this, what would you do if it happened?**

- **In a group, how can people be respectful of differing views or ideas? What if there are members who don't care what others think and want their views to drive the group's behavior?**

- **Why is it important for leaders to know how they feel and what they believe about issues that affect the group? If you don't know what you believe about something, how can you become aware and make a sound decision?**

- **Are there any statements you would take off the list? Why? Any you would add?**

VARIATION

If students contributed the statements, you may want to add a question or two such as:

- **How easy or difficult was it to come up with a statement that would prompt other group members to take a stand?**

- **Were there any statements you wanted to submit but didn't? Did you think the others wouldn't understand or would judge you? Explain.**

- **Do you feel there are any topics that are off limits in this group? In other groups? If so, what are they? Why do you feel these topics should be off limits?**

Wrapping Up

Remind teens to notice the day-to-day issues they feel strongly or are unsure about and to reflect on them. Encourage them to write in their notebooks or journals about personal convictions they hold and why they hold them. Suggest that they also write about issues they're undecided about as a way of exploring their values and clarifying their beliefs.

Extending the Learning

In this book, conduct the "Values Line" activity (pages 35–38) to delve deeper into personal values.

Have teens create posters. If you used the list of statements included on page 131, invite participants to write their own statements related to current social issues. If you conducted the "Variation," ask teens to write statements they could use with younger students. Then invite teens to choose from any of the statements (their own or those from this book) to create posters that vividly and succinctly state their views about the issues. Encourage participants to do research and include relevant facts or myths. Display the posters to get people outside the group thinking and talking.

Explore more issues and ideas. There are a number of books for finding statements that ask individuals to choose sides. You can refer to them to modify the statements for this activity or to prompt journal or essay writing in a language arts class. Since many of the books frame the issues as questions, you will need to recast them as statements. The books include:

101 Ethical Dilemmas by Martin Cohen (London: Routledge, 2007)

The Book of Questions by Gregory Stock (New York: Workman Publishing, 1987)

IF . . . Questions for Teens by Evelyn McFarlane and James Saywell (New York: Villard, 2001)

The Kids' Book of Questions: Revised for the New Century by Gregory Stock (New York: Workman Publishing, 2004)

More Would You Rather? Four Hundred and Sixty-Five More Provocative Questions to Get Teenagers Talking by Doug Fields (Grand Rapids, MI: Zondervan/Youth Specialties, 2005)

Statements for Choosing Sides

- Using alcohol and other drugs has become so common in our society that many people cannot make it through the day without them.

- People elected to lead countries are usually the best candidates for the job.

- Women have it easier in modern culture.

- How to treat immigrants is an important issue for many countries.

- Well-paid celebrities and famous athletes should be required to give some of their money to charity.

- Religion should be taught in school.

- Criminals can be changed and their past can be overcome.

- A cure for most cancers will be discovered in my lifetime.

- Advances in technology are the greatest inventions of all time.

- Men have it easier in modern culture.

- On a busy street, if a seemingly homeless person approached me and asked for money, I would give the person money.

- On a busy street, if a well-dressed stranger approached me and asked for money, I would give the person money.

- Years from now, if I discovered that there was a mix-up at the hospital and my wonderful one-year-old child was not mine, I would try to find the child's parent and exchange children to correct the mistake.

- If I found out that a good friend, sister, brother, or other person I love had AIDS, I would avoid that person.

- Years from now, at the time of my child's birth, if I could choose what his or her life would be like, I would.

- I have wished that I were of a different race.

- Stereotypes will always exist.

- I agree with everything my parents say.

- I agree with what is taught in school.

- I believe the world will be a better place 100 years from now.

- Advice from world and national leaders carries special weight because of their positions.

- My generation will have a positive and successful future.

- Given the chance to see the future, I would do so.

- I would do whatever it takes to become famous.

Add your own statements:

_____

_____

_____

_____

From *Teambuilding with Teens: Activities for Leadership, Decision Making, and Group Success* by Mariam G. MacGregor, M.S., copyright © 2008. Free Spirit Publishing Inc., Minneapolis, MN; www.freespirit.com. This page may be photocopied for individual, classroom, and group work only. For all other uses, call 800-735-7323.

Peace and Violence Webs

```
LEARNING CONCEPTS
```

- Awareness of social issues • Making a difference
- Critical thinking and social change

(40–60 MINUTES)

Peace and violence are universal issues that touch everyone deeply. Teens witness and experience first-hand the impact of terrorism, war, and social violence. This activity is designed to provoke discussion about both violence and peace and their effect on individuals and society. In groups of three, teens create two newsprint "web" posters about aspects of peace and violence. You will guide their work by prompting participants to consider questions about where both come from; how they are learned, expressed, and perpetuated; the impact they have; and how positive change can be brought about. After groups post their two webs side-by-side, discussion revolves around the similarities and differences between the two issues and the role individuals, groups, and leaders can have in effecting both.

GOALS

Participants will:

- explore the origins and impact of peace and violence in their lives
- identify ways individuals and groups can decrease and address violence
- identify ways individuals and groups can increase and perpetuate peace

MATERIALS NEEDED

- Newsprint
- Markers for all participants
- Masking tape

GETTING READY

On one sheet of newsprint, use a wide marker to write the following question prompts:

132

- Where does it come from?
- How do we learn it?
- Where do we see it?
- How does it impact society?
- Why and how does it continue?
- How can we make changes?

Hang the questions in a location where everyone can see them.

Separate two sheets of newsprint for each group of three teens. Place these in an area where participants can easily access them when it's time to begin the activity. Place the markers nearby.

Determine how you will divide the large group into smaller groups of three.

Setting the Stage

Teens are familiar with violence and peace in their lives and in the world around them. Everyone's experience is different, however, and you may have teens in your group who have had personal encounters with abuse, sexual assault, bullying, fighting or weaponry, torture, or other forms of violence. If these topics are sensitive to your group, you'll want to emphasize the importance of discussing them in a manner that values diverse perspectives while maintaining an atmosphere where teens feel comfortable sharing.

It's useful to take a few minutes at the start of the group meeting to explain that the group will be looking at the issues of peace and violence and that people have different views and experiences with both. In general, most teens are able to separate themselves from personal issues on these topics when working on the posters.

If conducting the activity in a group counseling setting, you will likely find that personal disclosure is more intense. Here you will want to remind teens in the group about confidentiality expectations and address the clinical aspects after the activity has been conducted.

Activity

Divide the large group into smaller groups of three teens each. Ask someone from each group to get two sheets of newsprint and three markers from the area where you've placed these items. Introduce the activity by saying:

Today you get a chance to think about two important issues that affect your life: peace and violence. Even though you all have experienced both, everyone has experienced them differently and may have different views about them. Keep that in mind as you work in your small groups.

First you will consider violence. On one of your sheets of newsprint, you'll write the word *violence* **in the middle. When you're done with this, you'll circle the word and draw lines coming from it. At the end of those lines, you'll write words that come to mind when you hear or think of violence. When you're finished you'll have a poster that shows a web about what violence is, where it comes from, what it looks like, and how it can be lessened.**

If you wish, draw a simple example of a peace or violence web structure on newsprint (see page 134). Then point to the questions you've posted and continue:

The questions on this poster can guide you in thinking about violence. Answering the questions can help you fill in your violence web.

Take 1–2 minutes to invite or share possible answers to each question. Examples might include the following:

- Where does it come from? *People can be born into it.*
- How do we learn it? *It can be learned in the family.*
- Where do we see it? *Gangs, media, music, wars.*
- How does it impact society? *It creates war and civil unrest.*
- Why and how does it continue? *Harsh discipline, child abuse, gangs.*
- How can we makes changes? *Learn how to deal with personal situations and conflict in safer, more respectful ways.*

You can write words about these questions or about other things that come to mind in your groups. You can also add more lines from the words you write, because one thing might make you think of another. You have 10 minutes to work on your violence webs. Any questions?

Section of a Sample Violence Web

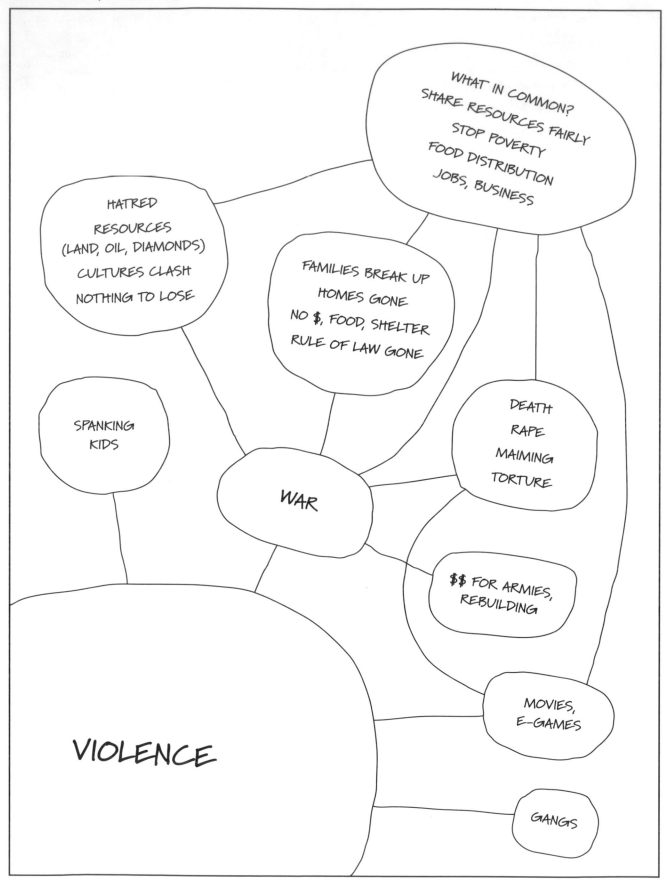

Briefly answer questions and then allow groups 10 minutes to work on their posters. Walk around the room to keep groups on task and to comment on the direction each group is taking. It can be a very interesting process and there is no "right" or "wrong" visual web. After 10 minutes, ask each group to briefly share their web. Tape up the webs, leaving space next to each for the peace webs that will come next. Then say:

Remain in your small groups. This time, on your second sheet of newsprint, you will write the word *peace* in the middle. You'll circle the word and draw lines coming from it. At the end of those lines, you'll write words that come to mind when you hear or think of peace. When you're finished you'll have a poster that shows a web about what peace is, where it comes from, what it looks like, and how it can be encouraged. The same questions you considered for your violence webs can help you as you think about peace and fill in your peace web.

Point again to the questions you have posted and take 1–2 minutes to invite or share possible answers to each. Examples might include the following:

- Where does it come from? *People can be born into it.*

- How do we learn it? *It can be learned in the family.*

- Where do we see it? *Symbols on clothing, media, music.*

- How does it impact society? *People get along, there's less violence.*

- Why and how does it continue? *How parents discipline, how friends work out differences.*

- How can we make changes? *Make sure we're choosing peaceful solutions to problems.*

You can write words about these questions or about other things that come to mind in your groups. You can also add more lines from the words you write, because one thing might make you think of another. You have 10 minutes to work on your peace webs. Any questions?

Briefly answer questions and then allow groups 10 minutes to work on their posters. Walk around the room to keep groups on task and to comment on the direction each group is taking. Here again there is no "right" or "wrong" visual web. After 10 minutes, ask each group to briefly share their web. Tape the peace webs next to the violence webs so people can look at them during the "Talk About It" discussion.

Talk About It

The activity and the conversations about the peace and violence webs can be stimulating. So that teens don't end the activity feeling overwhelmed by the issues, use the time remaining to dicuss questions like the following:

- **What do peace and violence have in common? What makes them different? Do you think violence will always exist? Will peace often be more difficult to achieve? Explain.**

- **Was one web easier to create than the other? Explain. What can you learn from this?**

- **Why do you think people often resort to violence to deal with problems? Why do you think peace is so much more difficult to achieve?**

- **What can individuals do to increase peace in their lives? Do you think this could impact peace and violence in society? Explain.**

- **If children grow up in violent surroundings, do you think it's natural that they will become violent themselves? How do you explain why some kids who *don't* grow up in violence still use violence to solve problems? Why do some kids who *do* grow up in violence turn to more peaceful approaches?**

- **What roles do leaders have in dealing with violence and promoting peace on a large scale? What roles do individuals play in doing this?**

If you're conducting this activity in a leadership-specific setting, you may want to frame the questions with greater leadership emphasis. Here are some questions you could ask:

- **Do you think countries at war can achieve peace after fighting?**

- **Can a leader who grew up surrounded by violence be trusted to promote peace for problem solving?**

- **There are many agencies in communities that deal with decreasing violence—the police, human services, prisons, and so forth—yet violence still occurs. What steps could leaders take to shift the emphasis on developing and promoting peace in an effort to decrease violent offenses?**

- **What can you do when you're in a leadership position to address the issues of peace and violence?**

Wrapping Up

If space allows, leave the posters hanging in the room or display them in the building hallways to prompt discussion among other teens. Otherwise, type or have a teen volunteer type the words, phrases, and ideas teens put on their peace and violence webs, and make copies to pass out. Encourage teens to observe their role in promoting peace or perpetuating violence and to consider ways they can serve as positive catalysts with their peers or as mentors for younger kids.

Extending the Learning

View and discuss movies. There are a number of appropriate films addressing peace and various aspects of violence (war, cultural issues, domestic issues, social issues). Since these resources are constantly changing, you can search through the Internet Movie Database (www.imdb.com) to find the most recent film releases. In the search box, choose "Keywords," and type "peace." The search will provide related keywords and help you narrow the film choices.

In this book, use the "Community Action Plan" (pages 143–147) activity to guide teens in undertaking a project addressing peace and violence.

Find more resources. You can find additional resources and lessons for discussing peace and violence, as well as ways teens can get involved with national and global organizations that promote peace, by checking out the following:

The Carter Center (www.cartercenter.org)
Founded by former U.S. President Jimmy Carter and former First Lady Rosalynn Carter, the Carter Center is dedicated to "waging peace by resolving conflicts, strengthening democracy, and advancing human rights worldwide." The center is involved in or sponsors a number of youth-specific programs and efforts around the world.

Free the Children (www.freethechildren.com)
This is the largest network of children helping children through education in the world, with more than one million youth involved in education and development programs in 45 countries. The organization's mission is to inspire young people to bring about positive social change to improve the lives of young people everywhere.

Idealist.org (www.idealist.org)
Idealist.org is a project of Action Without Borders, which connects people, organizations, and resources "to help build a world where all people can live free and dignified lives." Use the search boxes at the top of the page to find information on your topic of choice.

PeaceJam (www.peacejam.org)
The PeaceJam Foundation is dedicated to creating a new generation of young leaders committed to positive change in themselves, their communities, and the world through the inspiration of Nobel Peace Laureates, with whom annual youth workshops and weekend retreats take place. The Foundation provides five curricular programs that explore the stories of 12 Nobel Peace Laureates and the ways they overcame problems in their communities; you can access these programs through the Web site.

Wilderdom Experiential Education Activities (www.wilderdom.com/experiential)
A collection of activities, literature, and Web links focused on experiential learning.

Youth Service America (YSA) (www.ysa.org)
This resource center partners with thousands of organizations committed to increasing the quality and quantity of volunteer opportunities for young people ages 5–25 to serve locally, nationally, and globally. YSA envisions "a global culture of engaged youth committed to a lifetime of service, learning, leadership, and achievement," and is the coordinating organization of National and Global Youth Service Day.

Decision Making
and
Problem Solving

Bank Robbery

Community Action Plan

Challenges and Choices

Post Your Plans

The Million-Dollar Award

137

Bank Robbery

╔═══════════════════════════╗
 LEARNING CONCEPTS
╚═══════════════════════════╝

- Problem solving • Teamwork and group dynamics
- Communication skills

(25–40 MINUTES)

This activity is a fun way for groups of all ages to work through a problem that relies on every member's input for the solution. Each participant is given an essential piece of information about a fictional bank robbery that has taken place, and group members must work together, using the clues to solve the crime. The activity illustrates the importance of organization in group problem solving and highlights ways the group can improve their teamwork to solve real problems they may encounter in the future. At the same time, it reinforces the fact that all team members have something valuable to contribute and that it is important to consider everyone's viewpoints, ideas, and information when problem solving.

GOALS

Participants will:

- learn to involve and rely on all members to accomplish a task
- strengthen communication and teamwork skills in a group setting
- clarify how to solve problems and achieve goals despite possible roadblocks

MATERIALS NEEDED

- Scissors
- Handouts: "Bank Robbery Clues" (pages 140–141) and "Bank Robbery Key" (page 142)

GETTING READY

Make two copies of the "Bank Robbery Clues." Keep one for your reference; cut the other into individual clues, one for each group member. Fold the clues in half to hide the information on each slip. Enough clues are included for a group of 28. If you have fewer members, double up some clues so that random members receive more than one clue. If you wish, you can remove the last four clues for a total of 24 clues. Although not essential, the last four serve to further complicate the picture as teens work to solve the mystery. If your group has more than 28 members, have one teen serve as a timekeeper and any others as observers.

If you wish, make a copy of the "Bank Robbery Key" for yourself.

Organize the chairs in a large circle so teens can see one another.

Activity

When teens arrive, ask them to sit on a chair in the circle. Do not ask the teams to designate a leader. Explain the activity like this:

> You have just learned that a neighborhood bank in New York City has been robbed of one million dollars. This group is the detective team that is investigating the robbery and attempting to identify the thief or thieves. Each of the slips of paper I'm holding contains a clue about what happened. If you put all the facts together, you'll solve the mystery.
>
> There are a few rules to follow so the investigation is not compromised. First, you can organize the chairs in any way you want, but you're to remain in your seats—you may not get up and walk around the group while you're working. Second, you need to share the information in your clue orally—by talking. No passing clues around or showing them to anyone else, and no writing them anywhere either! Remember, everyone's clue is important.
>
> In addition to learning who committed the robbery, you need to figure out the alibis of the other people being investigated—where they actually were at the time the bank was robbed. Anytime the entire group agrees that it has an answer, you can tell me. If you're right, I'll tell you. If not, I will only tell you *whether* your answers are *in*correct—not *which* ones are wrong. You'll have 25 minutes to talk together and try to solve the crime.

Answer any questions and then pass out the clues, making sure that people don't show them to others in the group.

If your group has observers, allow them to make minor suggestions to the group about how they can work together more effectively, but remind them not to suggest ideas about the solution.

As facilitator, stand unobtrusively outside the group and indicate every 5 minutes of time that passes. You may want to jot notes about the group's organization, how it works together, stumbling blocks, communication styles, and so forth. Refer to these when the group discusses the experience during "Talk About It."

Regardless of whether the group solves the mystery, end the process after 25 minutes. Allow teens a few minutes to go around the circle and share their clues. If the group didn't solve the crime, share the actual solution before discussing what happened during the activity.

Talk About It

Take 10–15 minutes to talk about the activity. Consider these discussion questions related to the group's experience:

- How did your way of working together change as the activity went along? What would you do in real life if the same thing were happening in a group you're a member of?

- If you figured out the mystery, was it easy or hard to do so? How did your group come up with the answer? If the group didn't figure out the mystery, what needed to happen in order for you to do so?

- Was a leader needed to accomplish this goal? If yes, who emerged as a leader? (Talk about how this leader emerged.) If not, what does this tell you about how your group solves problems without a leader?

- How did it feel to *need* every single person to take part in solving the crime? Was anyone overlooked or did anyone dominate the process? How did this affect your group's success? What steps can be taken to make sure everyone on your team is included when working toward a certain goal?

- What happened when someone forgot a clue or made an incorrect connection between clues? How did your group communicate and react in this situation?

- Were there any moments when you wanted to cheat—for example, by passing around the clues, laying them out in order, or walking around to see other people's clues? Why did you or didn't you do this? How does this relate to real-life situations where you receive clear instructions on what is acceptable for accomplishing a goal?

- If this had been an important real-life situation, how well would the team have done? Explain.

Wrapping Up

Encourage teens to observe the ways they solve problems when participating as individual members of a group. Also ask them to notice how people are included or excluded when decisions are made. Remind them to keep in mind what they've learned about listening to and counting on all members of the group and to apply it the next time the team encounters a decision-making situation.

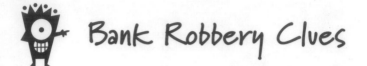

Bank Robbery Clues

The robbery was discovered at 8:00 a.m. on Friday. The bank had closed at 5:00 p.m. on Thursday evening.

Margaret Charity, a teller at the bank, discovered the robbery.

The vault of the bank had been blasted open by dynamite.

The president of the bank, Mr. Moneybags, left before the robbery was discovered. Authorities at the Mexico City airport arrested him at noon on Friday.

The president of the bank had been arguing with his wife about money. He had talked frequently about leaving her.

The front door of the bank had been opened with a key.

The janitor and the president of the bank possess the only keys to the bank.

Margaret Charity often borrowed the president's key to open the bank early when she had an extra amount of work to do.

A strange person had been hanging around the bank on Thursday, watching employees and customers.

A large amount of dynamite had been stolen from the Acme Construction Company on Wednesday.

An Acme Construction Company employee, George Charity, said that a strange person had been hanging around the construction company on Wednesday afternoon.

The strange person who had been hanging around the bank and the construction company is John Rosales. John Rosales had recently dropped out of New York University and was found by police in East Baystream, about 10 miles from New York City.

John Rosales was carrying $500 when police apprehended him. He had thrown something into the river as the police approached.

Aimee Chang of East Baystream told police that she had bought $500 worth of genuine antique glass beads from John Rosales, and that she planned to resell them in her boutique in downtown East Baystream.

MORE

From *Teambuilding with Teens: Activities for Leadership, Decision Making, and Group Success* by Mariam G. MacGregor, M.S., copyright © 2008. Free Spirit Publishing Inc., Minneapolis, MN; www.freespirit.com. This page may be photocopied for individual, classroom, and group work only. For all other uses, call 800-735-7323.

Aimee Chang said that John Rosales had spent Thursday night at her parents' home and left after a pleasant breakfast on Friday morning.

When police tried to locate the custodian of the bank, Peter Smith, he apparently had disappeared.

Margaret Charity stated that her brother, George, had seen Peter Smith running from the bank as George was strolling to the 24-Hour Diner for coffee around eleven o'clock Thursday night.

The FBI in Atlantic City, New Jersey, found Peter Smith on Friday. He had arrived there by train at five o'clock Thursday evening.

The train conductor confirmed the time of Peter Smith's arrival.

Mr. Moneybags is the only person who has a key to the vault.

There were no trains out of Atlantic City between 4:00 p.m. Thursday and 7:00 a.m. Friday.

In addition to keeping payroll records, George Charity is in charge of the dynamite supplies of the Acme Construction Company.

Margaret Charity said that Peter Smith had often flirted with her.

Mr. Moneybags waited in the terminal at the Los Angeles airport for 16 hours because of engine trouble on the plane he was to take to Mexico City.

Mr. Moneybags's brother, John Poorman, had always been jealous of his brother.

John Poorman is known to always go to a movie on Friday nights.

John Poorman appeared in Los Angeles on Monday waving a lot of money.

John Poorman wanted to marry Peter Smith's sister.

From *Teambuilding with Teens: Activities for Leadership, Decision Making, and Group Success* by Mariam G. MacGregor, M.S., copyright © 2008. Free Spirit Publishing Inc., Minneapolis, MN; www.freespirit.com. This page may be photocopied for individual, classroom, and group work only. For all other uses, call 800-735-7323.

Bank Robbery Key

The Charitys worked together to rob the bank. **Margaret Charity** supplied the front-door key that she had borrowed from **Mr. Moneybags**. Her brother, **George Charity**, supplied the dynamite.

Mr. Moneybags had already left for Mexico when the robbery took place.

Peter Smith was already in Atlantic City on the night of the robbery. **The Charitys** were lying when they tried to frame him for the robbery.

John Rosales was at **Aimee Chang's** parents' house.

There was no evidence that **Mr. Moneybags's** brother **John Poorman** had anything to do with the robbery.

From *Teambuilding with Teens: Activities for Leadership, Decision Making, and Group Success* by Mariam G. MacGregor, M.S., copyright © 2008. Free Spirit Publishing Inc., Minneapolis, MN; www.freespirit.com. This page may be photocopied for individual, classroom, and group work only. For all other uses, call 800-735-7323.

Community Action Plan

(45 MINUTES)

Often, teen leaders are so excited to undertake group projects that they overlook the specifics of setting goals and organizing the project plan. When this happens, they may have a difficult time getting their project underway or keeping it on track. "Community Action Plan" is designed to help teen leaders and groups identify, prioritize, and undertake appropriate steps for any project. Especially helpful for committees and small groups, the activity and planning format are also effective for individual and large-group use. With the planning form as a guide, groups work through a five-step process to establish a blueprint to prepare for, execute, and evaluate their project. Use the activity as an exercise for structuring group projects and to assist teens in designing specific leadership, community, or service projects. The 45-minute time frame is to complete the project plan—project implementation and follow-through will require additional time.

GOALS

Participants will:

- identify and agree upon a group goal
- identify issues and priorities for a group project
- establish steps to plan and evaluate a group project

MATERIALS NEEDED

- Pen or pencil for each participant
- Handout: "Community Action Plan" (pages 145–147)
- *Optional*—Additional blank sheets of paper as needed

143

GETTING READY

How the group uses the planning form will vary depending on the project they will undertake. Be prepared to introduce the activity as it relates to the project or objective they will address.

Make a copy of the "Community Action Plan" handout for each teen. Determine how you will use the planner and whether and how the group will be divided. (For more on organizing the group, see "Setting the Stage.")

Setting the Stage

If you will be having teens divide into smaller groups or committees, you might want to conduct a brainstorming session at the beginning of the activity for teens to identify the projects they'll be working on. If they will be working on a large group project that has already been identified, you can skip the brainstorming session and have them work through the "Community Action Plan" planning form with the guidance of their teen group leader or by inviting a teen volunteer to guide the process.

During the preliminary process, it may be helpful for groups working on one large project to begin to identify committees. Each of these committees can use relevant sections of the handout to guide their discussions and pinpoint their specific responsibilities.

Activity

Introduce the activity as it relates to your group's project. Pass out a copy of the "Community Action Plan" to each teen. Before having teens work through the form, read through it together to highlight specifics of each step and answer any questions.

Allow teens to work together through the steps on the form. You may need to assist with keeping a large group or small groups on task. Suggest that they first go through the form with a broad outlook, considering the big picture. Once they've accomplished this, assist them in revisiting it to determine the specifics, including due dates and individual assignments and responsibilities. Teens may want to keep track of information on separate sheets of paper as necessary. It's important for members to see and develop their plan as a working document, one they'll refer to, revise, and fine-tune as they undertake and follow through on their project.

Allow up to 40 minutes for teens to work through the planner. When they've completed it, help them determine how they will follow the plan they've set and when time will be allotted for them to revisit and update it throughout their project.

Talk About It

This activity may not require additional discussion. If you want to discuss the planning process and what participants learned from it, consider discussion questions like these:

- **What new things did you learn about everyone's view of the goals of your group?**

- **As you planned, how did you use the strengths and talents of the group? As you move forward to work on your project, how will you make the most of people's strengths and talents and still allow everyone a chance to try new things or use new talents when working together?**

- **How could you use this planning form for an individual project?**

Extending the Learning

Debrief after the project is completed. If your group proceeds with their plan and carries out a project, take time at the end of the process to consider these discussion questions:

- **During your project, did your group revisit the plan you made? How did it help keep you on track? How did the plan change as you went along?**

- **In what ways did going through the steps on the "Community Action Plan" at the beginning help your project's success?**

Community Action Plan

Step 1: Identify your issue.

What is the school or community issue we want to address?

_____

_____

Why is the issue important to our group? Why is it important to our community, school, program, or organization?

_____

_____

_____

Step 2: Brainstorm.

What is our plan, project, or strategy to make a difference? What do we want to accomplish?

_____

_____

_____

How and why will our plan make a difference with this issue? (What change will occur? Are people ready for a change? How will they react?)

_____

_____

_____

How can we determine if this plan, project, or strategy is necessary, will make a difference, and can be successful? Possible ideas:

_____ Number of interested volunteers   _____ Pre-project surveys

_____ Support from adult staff   _____ Ease of raising money

_____ Number we think will attend   _____ Community interest

_____ Previous success with similar project   _____ Exciting new idea

_____ _____   _____ _____
          (other ideas)   (other ideas)   **MORE** ➡

From *Teambuilding with Teens: Activities for Leadership, Decision Making, and Group Success* by Mariam G. MacGregor, M.S., copyright © 2008. Free Spirit Publishing Inc., Minneapolis, MN; www.freespirit.com. This page may be photocopied for individual, classroom, and group work only. For all other uses, call 800-735-7323.

Step 3: Come up with specific ideas for carrying out your plan.

What skills or knowledge must we learn to make our project happen? What skills do we already have as a team?

_____

_____

How will we learn the new skills or knowledge we're missing?

_____

_____

What resources (money, time, materials) and support will we need?

_____

_____

How will we get these resources and support? Be specific. (Who is responsible for what? How will we keep track of materials and details?)

_____

_____

If our project involves helping other people, how will we gain their participation, interest, and input?

_____

_____

What other individuals, groups, or organizations can help with our project?

_____

_____

How will we involve and recognize these other groups for their contributions?

_____

_____

From *Teambuilding with Teens: Activities for Leadership, Decision Making, and Group Success* by Mariam G. MacGregor, M.S., copyright © 2008. Free Spirit Publishing Inc., Minneapolis, MN; www.freespirit.com. This page may be photocopied for individual, classroom, and group work only. For all other uses, call 800-735-7323.

When and where will we implement our plan?

_____

_____

Does our project need an alternative plan in case of bad weather or other possible challenges? If so, what is it?

_____

_____

What specific parts and steps need to be assigned to group members? (List these and assign the responsible person.) Does everyone agree to their assignments? What are the specific due dates for each part of the project or plan? Be specific.

_____

_____

Step 5: Determine how you will evaluate your project.

How will we know we've been successful? Possible ideas:

_____ Post-project surveys   _____ Evaluation form for participants

_____ Objective observers   _____ Amount of money raised

_____ Number of attendees   _____ Newspaper and media coverage

_____ Group evaluation   _____ Post-project discussion

_____ Individual evaluation   _____ Teacher/adult sponsor feedback

Other steps or tools to evaluate our final outcome:

_____

_____

_____

From *Teambuilding with Teens: Activities for Leadership, Decision Making, and Group Success* by Mariam G. MacGregor, M.S., copyright © 2008. Free Spirit Publishing Inc., Minneapolis, MN; www.freespirit.com. This page may be photocopied for individual, classroom, and group work only. For all other uses, call 800-735-7323.

Challenges and Choices

LEARNING CONCEPTS

- Decision making • Personal values
- Understanding ethics and ethical behavior

(45 MINUTES)

Ethics and ethical decision making can be a challenging topic to address with teens because of their growing awareness of the inconsistencies of ethical behavior modeled by leaders and others in power around them. This activity allows teens to privately evaluate their personal ethics by taking an inventory, to discuss these attitudes at their own comfort level, and to explore, as a group, the gray areas involved in making ethical decisions. This activity is best used after having established common understanding of ethics and how these relate to decision making. The activity is a good fit with school-to-career subject matter or can be used in conjunction with other ethics discussions or activities in a wide range of settings. There is also an extension activity for establishing codes of behavior for the overall group. Plan an additional meeting of 30–45 minutes if you wish to develop a group code of ethics.

GOALS

Participants will:

- learn how they apply ethics when making decisions

- identify similarities and differences in the group regarding ethical values and behaviors

- explore how "What if?" questions can affect ethical decisions

- consider or develop a code of ethics for guiding group decisions

MATERIALS NEEDED

- Pen or pencil for each participant

- Handouts: "Ethical Choices Inventory" and "Ethical Choices Score Summaries" (pages 152–154)

Setting the Stage

Making ethical decisions, whether personal or as part of a group, is never easy. Some teens may have a concrete sense of what to do in most situations, relying on black-and-white rules or results. Others may feel unprepared or unable to choose between difficult choices that appear "gray." At times, too, teens may simply want to act on the first thought that comes to mind, regardless of how wise or unwise it may be. By taking time to establish personal guidelines for weighing the issues involved, teens can learn how to do what's most right in many circumstances or dilemmas they face through adolescence and young adulthood. The guidelines they begin to form now will also serve them well throughout life.

Depending on the developmental level of group members, dealing with issues of right and wrong can lead to heated debates. This is especially true if some teens are still in concrete thinking stages and not yet ready to apply learning more abstractly. Teens who are still concrete thinkers tend to believe that there are cut-and-dry answers to most issues and that people should stick firmly to laws or rules set by parents, government, school, work, or religious institutions. Abstract thinkers are capable of recognizing that decisions have personal repercussions; these students will likely be more willing to explore the vague areas that make many dilemmas complex to resolve.

Making ethical decisions calls for balancing personal values with the needs of others. In group situations, it means respecting everyone's values and acting with integrity in an attempt to do what's right for the group. Taking time to evaluate one's personal views about making decisions in challenging situations contributes to being able to stand on solid ground once a decision is made. As a facilitator, you will want to be sensitive to young or undeveloped attitudes about integrity and ethics, carefully guiding the discussion so teens can understand, practice, and address ethical dilemmas in real or hypothetical situations.

In the activity, teens tally their inventory scores, and it's up to you to determine whether you will invite them to share their scores with others during the group discussion. Sharing scores among group members can be an uncomfortable step, especially for teens who find themselves with a lower score than their peers. Thus, determine if challenging the comfort zone of these individuals is something you want to accomplish through this particular lesson on ethics. You might find that such a challenge is the reason for conducting the activity and that therefore pointed discussion about individual behavior is appropriate, or you might want to allow learning to take place internally, without exposure to peer opinions.

Activity

If your group hasn't yet discussed the meaning of ethics, do so briefly at the start of the activity. A simple definition is this: "Ethics is deciding what is right—or most right—in any situation, especially when there's no clear answer." Invite teens to offer examples of ethical dilemmas they've faced. You might suggest some possible examples such as excluding information on a college application, reporting a friend who's done something illegal, or taking certain risks with unknown outcomes.

Tell participants that they will now have a chance to consider how they feel about different issues of ethics. Explain that what guides them in personal ethical situations can be called a "code of ethics," which is like an honor code they expect themselves to live by.

Pass out a copy of the "Ethical Choices Inventory" to each teen. Ask participants to complete the handouts privately, without sharing their responses or discussing the questions with others. As individuals complete their inventories, ask them to stay quiet until everyone is done. Allow about 10 minutes for this.

When everyone has completed and tallied the inventories, pass out a copy of the "Ethical Choices Score

After teens have determined their scores, read through each item on the inventory and spend a few minutes discussing the meaning and application in their lives. This is a time to explore the complexity of making ethical choices. Discuss the fact that decisions can seem okay in certain situations, yet completely wrong in others. Challenge teens to consider "What if?" scenarios in regard to some of the items on the inventory. (For example, for item 1, "When applying to colleges, I wouldn't include any disciplinary action I've faced at school or a job," ask: "What if the disciplinary action was the result of a misunderstanding, and you feel it was unfair?") Invite teens to volunteer their perspectives on the different items. Since the inventory responses are personal, teens may not wish to share their specific answers with the large group. Similarly, depending on the dynamics of your group and the nature of their membership, you may or may not want to invite participants to share their scores and discuss their feelings about the summaries.

Talk About It

Use 10–15 minutes to have the group consider these discussion questions:

- **How can completing the "Ethical Choices Inventory" help you think about and prepare for situations you'll face from now on?**

- **Can you think of a recent situation where your code of ethics was challenged? How did you deal with the situation? How did your decision affect others who were involved?**

- **In what situations (or with what people) do you feel like your intent to act ethically is challenged the most? Explain.**

- **Can you think of a local, national, or international event where the individuals or groups involved had to make ethical decisions? How did people behave? What choices did they make? Do you think they should have done anything differently to make better ethical decisions? Explain.**

- **Do you think a person can be a good leader or group member without being ethical? Explain.**

Wrapping Up

Allow teens to keep their inventories and score summaries. Suggest that they use them to continue to reflect on and write down their own code of ethics in their notebooks or journals. Explain that a personal ethical code can help them determine what is right or wrong (or good or bad) based on their own values—on the things that are important to them and their family or group. With a code of ethics, they'll have guidelines on which to base decisions that aren't so clear or that involve less-than-desirable alternatives.

Extending the Learning

Develop a group code of ethics. Plan a follow-up meeting for teens to work in small groups to develop a group code of ethics, using the "Creating a Group Code of Ethics" handout on page 155. You might refer to this as your group's honor code, a phrase that's familiar to many teens in a school setting. Have teens work in small teams of three to five people, making notes on their handouts and using newsprint to summarize their responses to the questions about personal and group values. The questions on the form about personal ethics are included so group members can be aware of the values of everyone in the group as they consider collective values. Hang the sheets around the room to use for discussion and comparison, and invite each group to briefly explain their ideas. Then shift from small teams back to the large group to write an overall "Group Code of Ethics" that can be used to guide the group through the time they will continue meeting and working together. Encourage participants to incorporate ideas from each small group into the code the entire group can agree with. If the group has established teen leaders, consider having them guide and facilitate the process of writing the code.

Have teens explore ethics case studies. Doing this is particularly helpful and enjoyable because teens can compare their responses or attitudes with those of their peers. Here are several resources for case studies:

Institute for Global Ethics (www.globalethics.org)
This is an independent, nonsectarian, nonpartisan, non-profit organization that promotes ethical action and provides numerous case studies to use with young people and adults. At the Web site, choose "Dilemmas" to find a variety of case studies in different settings.

Society of Professional Journalists (www.spj.org)
Particularly useful for writing, journalism classes, or teen newspaper staffs, this resource presents real-life ethical case studies for debate and discussion. Choose "Ethics" to find case studies and links to articles and interviews of journalists and high-profile writers who've dealt with ethics in their line of work.

University of San Diego Ethics Updates (http://ethics.sandiego.edu)
This Web site, founded and edited by Lawrence M. Hinman, is designed primarily to be used by ethics instructors and their students. It provides resources and updates on current literature, both popular and professional, that relates to ethics.

Some books to consider include those listed in the "Choosing Sides" activity (page 130) as well as these:

Aesop's Fables, available in various editions, is a classic resource for discussing situations and decisions that are morally and ethically grounded.

The Conscience of the Campus: Case Studies in Moral Reasoning Among Today's College Students by Joseph Dillon Davey and Linda DuBois Davey (Westport, CT: Praeger Paperbacks, 2001). Though written for an older population, this is useful with teen groups ready for applying ethical decision making with greater abstraction to real-life situations.

"Making Ethical Decisions: The Basic Primer on Using the Six Pillars of Character to Make Better Decisions and a Better Life" by Michael S. Josephson (Los Angeles: Josephson Institute of Ethics, 2002). This easy-to-read booklet includes realistic examples and a step-by-step decision-making model.

They Broke the Law—You Be the Judge: True Cases of Teen Crime by Thomas A. Jacobs (Minneapolis: Free Spirit Publishing, 2003). Judge Jacobs lets teen readers "preside" over real-life cases of teens in trouble and then learn what the actual judge decided and where the offenders are today. Related role plays and scenarios can be downloaded at www.freespirit.com.

What Would We Do If . . . by Shalmarie Bunker and Kim Osborne (Springville, UT: Bonneville Books, 2003). Written for parents, the situations and scripts can be adapted easily for use in many different situations; chapters present real-life circumstances at home, friends' homes, school, and in the community that prepare kids of all ages to make solid, grounded decisions.

What Would You Do? Quizzes About Real Life Problems by Patti Kelley Criswell (Middleton, WI: American Girl Publishing, 2004). Written for tween girls.

To identify movies that address ethics and to find discussion outlines related to those films, visit Teach with Movies (www.teachwithmovies.org). Because new films are released regularly, the site may not include discussion outlines for some more current movies. Click on "Search TWM" on the main page to find appropriate movies using the search box or the site's twelve indexes.

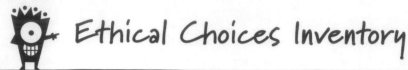 Ethical Choices Inventory

Describe how well you agree with each of the following statements, based on this scale:

5 Disagree Strongly   **4** Disagree   **3** Neutral   **2** Agree   **1** Agree Strongly

_____ 1. When applying to colleges, I would not mention any disciplinary action I've faced at school or a job.

_____ 2. When shopping, if the clerk rings up the sale wrong and doesn't charge me enough, I don't see a reason to tell him or her.

_____ 3. Students should not inform on each other for wrongdoing, such as cheating.

_____ 4. When getting reimbursed for money spent for my club or team, it's okay to write up a fake receipt that looks like the real thing if the original receipt gets lost.

_____ 5. I see no problem with doing personal things (talking on the phone, writing emails) when I'm supposed to be doing work for my group project.

_____ 6. I think it is okay to exaggerate about what I'm capable of doing so I get chosen for a certain position, project, or job.

_____ 7. I think it's okay for businesses (stores, advertisers, etc.) to stretch the truth about when a product will be ready or delivered just to get me as a customer.

_____ 8. Flirting with someone in a decision-making position (like a group leader or boss) just to get something I want (like certain position or a raise) is okay.

_____ 9. If I were paid a lot of cash for my after-school job, and my employer gave me no record of my payment, I would not report the money I earned on my government tax form.

_____ 10. I see no harm in taking home a few office supplies or items from my club, organization, or job.

_____ 11. It's okay to read email messages, check text messages, or listen to voicemails of others, even when not invited to do so.

_____ 12. It's acceptable to call in sick in order to take a day off.

 Adapted from "The Ethical Reasoning Inventory" by Dr. Andrew DuBrin in *The Complete Idiot's Guide to Leadership, 2nd edition* (Alpha Books, 2000). Adapted and reprinted with permission from Dr. Andrew DuBrin. From *Teambuilding with Teens: Activities for Leadership, Decision Making, and Group Success* by Mariam G. MacGregor, M.S., copyright © 2008. Free Spirit Publishing Inc., Minneapolis, MN; www.freespirit.com. This page may be photocopied for individual, classroom, and group work only. For all other uses, call 800-735-7323.

_____ 13. I would accept a year-long job or leadership position for my club, group, or team, even if I knew I was planning on keeping it for only a couple of months.

_____ 14. I would accept an expensive gift from a person (or from people, a college, a coach) who may have influence on how I do things without first checking my school or team rules.

_____ 15. To be successful, a person usually has to ignore ethics and integrity.

_____ 16. If I felt physically attracted toward a person running for a leadership position, I would choose that person over a more qualified candidate.

_____ 17. When I'm with others, I always go along with their ideas even if I'm not being honest.

_____ 18. It's okay to copy or download software, music, games, and other copyrighted material without authorized permission from the producer or publisher.

_____ 19. I think it is okay to take home an item from the store for a 30-day trial, even if I have no intention of buying it.

_____ 20. I would accept credit for someone else's ideas.

_____ **Total Score** (add all answers)

Adapted from "The Ethical Reasoning Inventory" by Dr. Andrew DuBrin in *The Complete Idiot's Guide to Leadership, 2nd edition* (Alpha Books, 2000). Adapted and reprinted with permission from Dr. Andrew DuBrin. From *Teambuilding with Teens: Activities for Leadership, Decision Making, and Group Success* by Mariam G. MacGregor, M.S., copyright © 2008. Free Spirit Publishing Inc., Minneapolis, MN; www.freespirit.com. This page may be photocopied for individual, classroom, and group work only. For all other uses, call 800-735-7323.

Ethical Choices Score Summaries

Use these descriptions to understand your score on the "Ethical Choices Inventory."

90–100   You have a strong sense of ethics with clear ideas about what's right or wrong. Friends may joke or tease you about being a "goody-goody," but you're also seen as having exceptional integrity and people know you're always true to your word.

60–89   Your sense of ethics continues to develop. At times you question generally accepted values or you don't feel strongly about them. Depending on the people you're with or the situation you face, you may find yourself struggling to make a firm decision because you recognize a lot of gray areas and "What if?" questions. Keep challenging yourself to understand and work through difficult issues so you will be able to make clear choices and decisions.

41–59   You have some awareness about ethical issues. You struggle with making decisions when faced with difficult choices, sometimes making choices with negative consequences. At times you may not see why some generally accepted values are important. Challenge yourself to look more closely at the reasons behind your choices and behind social guidelines. Working toward a more clear sense of ethics will help you make better decisions.

40 or below   Your sense of ethics is not in line with general expectations of society. This may have led you to make choices that had negative consequences, and it is likely to create more problems as you face new decisions. Working to build a stronger sense of ethics will leave you feeling more confident about the choices you make. You may also be discouraged or confused. Consider talking with a trusted adult or respected peer about your feelings and attitudes to help you find ways to feel more connected.

 Adapted from "The Ethical Reasoning Inventory" by Dr. Andrew DuBrin in *The Complete Idiot's Guide to Leadership, 2nd edition* (Alpha Books, 2000). Adapted and reprinted with permission from Dr. Andrew DuBrin. From *Teambuilding with Teens: Activities for Leadership, Decision Making, and Group Success* by Mariam G. MacGregor, M.S., copyright © 2008. Free Spirit Publishing Inc., Minneapolis, MN; www.freespirit.com. This page may be photocopied for individual, classroom, and group work only. For all other uses, call 800-735-7323.

Creating a Group Code of Ethics

To Begin

Start by considering your own personal standards of right and wrong. What expectations do you have of yourself that guide you in everyday life? (*examples:* always doing your best in everything you do, keeping promises, putting family first) Jot down some words or phrases that describe your personal attitudes:

_____

_____

_____

The Next Step

Now consider the rules and standards—both written and unwritten—that apply to your group. When serving as a member of your group, how are you expected to act? (*examples:* expected to say certain things when representing the group, expected to promote particular ideas on behalf of the group) Jot down some words or phrases that describe the expectations about the group as a whole and the attitudes and values the group considers important:

_____

_____

_____

Putting It Together

Consider how these two sets of values and expectations fit together. Do people's personal standards and group standards work well together? How do they conflict? What needs to change to make them consistent and to have them positively support one another? Jot down any ideas that seem helpful:

_____

_____

_____

Use these ideas to work with the large group to create a "Group Code of Ethics" to guide the behavior and decision making of people as individuals and as members of your group.

From *Teambuilding with Teens: Activities for Leadership, Decision Making, and Group Success* by Mariam G. MacGregor, M.S., copyright © 2008. Free Spirit Publishing Inc., Minneapolis, MN; www.freespirit.com. This page may be photocopied for individual, classroom, and group work only. For all other uses, call 800-735-7323.

Post Your Plans

- Decision making
- Setting goals and creating vision
- Developing a group project
- Teamwork and group dynamics

(45 MINUTES)

Self-adhesive notes provide a medium that makes this goal-setting activity engaging and energizing. Teens create overall priorities for their group and work in small groups to identify specific action steps that will help achieve these goals, writing their ideas on self-stick notes. Then, in the large group, they post their plans on newsprint, discuss the ideas, and move different goals and steps around as the large group focuses and organizes their priorities. The process creates a large visual to support the direction and objectives of the group. While basic goal setting can be accomplished quickly, more comprehensive planning can take several sessions, making this an effective activity for a weekend retreat. If the group has identified a teen leader, that person can serve as co-facilitator with you. You will need a good deal of wall space. The 45-minute time period allows for basic goal setting. Plan 50–55 minutes if using the "Variation," and plan additional 45-minute meetings for ongoing or lengthy goal setting.

GOALS

Participants will:

- work with group members to identify goals and priorities
- identify specific action steps needed to achieve group goals and priorities
- create a working document to guide the group toward their objectives

MATERIALS NEEDED

- Large pad of newsprint
- Markers
- Masking tape
- Pen or pencil for each participant
- Self-adhesive note pads, one for each small group
- Handout: "What Are Action Steps?" (page 160)
- *Optional*—17" x 22" copier paper

GETTING READY

Separate the newsprint from the pad so it is easier to pass out. Hang six sheets of newsprint across an open wall. The remaining sheets should be in a location where you can access them to pass out to the small groups along with the self-stick notepads and pens or pencils.

Make a copy of "What Are Action Steps?" on 17" x 22" paper (set the copy ratio at 200%) or use a marker to rewrite the information on a sheet of newsprint. Have this handy to hang on the wall when the groups start working through action steps.

Determine how you will divide the large group into smaller groups to brainstorm action steps.

Depending on your group and the goals you anticipate, you may want to allow teens to choose the goals they'd like to focus on or you may decide to assign groups based on how you think they will best function. (If working with a teen leader, do this with his or her input.)

Setting the Stage

Finding interesting and engaging ways for groups to set and evaluate goals can be a challenge. Often, groups skip over the process because it can be boring and burdensome. As a result, teens lose interest before they've even put their goals into action plans! The interactive nature of this activity gives energy to this task and typically generates lots of good ideas. Because of this, and because the activity is geared toward identifying specific outcomes for the group, no additional time is needed for a separate "Talk About It" discussion. Teens will leave the meetings with specific results and actions to take, and they won't necessarily need to discuss what they thought of the process. This can take place informally outside the group's regular meeting time.

Activity

Introduce the idea of determining group goals and action steps based on the group's experience doing this. You might use words like the following, tailoring them to the purpose of the group:

Today you are going to work on setting this group's goals and deciding specific action steps you'll take in order to achieve those goals. *Goals* **and** *action steps* **are two different things. The** *goals* **of the group are the big-picture priorities you have for the time you will work together.** (This might be over the upcoming year, semester, month, project, or other parameter.) **For example, because you are a (**student council**), your priorities might include (**promoting spirit and involvement at school or undertaking a service project**). The** *action steps* **to support or accomplish those priorities are the specific tasks needed to get the job done. For example, the action steps for (**promoting spirit**) could include (**creating school T-shirts for each season or planning a school movie night**). Are there any questions about the difference between goals and action steps?**

Allow a few minutes to respond to questions, making sure to reinforce that goals are the overall priorities and action steps are specific tasks that support the goals. Another analogy you can use is that goals are like headings on a term paper and action steps are the facts and research supporting the message of your paper. When teens are clear about the differences, continue by saying:

Your first step is to identify the group's goals or priorities. To do this, I will lead you in a 5-minute brainstorming session. Think about the general areas this group would like to focus on. What are the most important things you want to accomplish?

Using one of the six sheets of newsprint, write or have a teen volunteer write down the ideas teens call out. Examples of priorities for a student council might include the following (this is not an exhaustive list):

- leadership development
- increased school participation in activities
- improved public relations
- community service projects
- committee responsibilities
- social activities and projects (such as homecoming, prom, carnivals)
- recruitment of new members
- fundraising

Examples of priorities for a youth advisory board might include the following (this is not an exhaustive list):

- leadership development
- communication among members
- improved adult-youth relationships

- recruitment of new members (youth and adult)
- community service projects
- promoting the work of the advisory board
- developing policy
- training adults working with youth

These are just sample lists; since every group is different, the brainstorming can be quite extensive. During brainstorming you'll want to remain open to a broad range of ideas; if necessary, point out when action steps are brought up rather than goals, and keep the focus on goals and priorities. You may want to hang up another sheet of newsprint where you can jot down any great action-step ideas that arise so the group can refer to those later.

After 5 minutes, ask the group to talk together to identify the top five priorities from the list. Allow 5–10 minutes for them to do this. When they are done, write a single priority on each of the remaining five sheets of newsprint hanging on the wall. If the group has brainstormed a very large list of goals, consider conducting the variation to summarize the top five priorities. This will require an additional 5–10 minutes.

VARIATION

If the group has come up with a large number of priorities, or if they will be meeting indefinitely and will revisit goals through their time together, the process of narrowing down priorities can be difficult. To accomplish this and allow everyone's voice to be heard, use this process:

Pass out five sticky notes to each teen. Ask participants to individually review the newsprint with the brainstormed list of priorities, identify what they consider the top five priorities, write one priority on each sticky note, and affix the notes to the five blank sheets of newsprint. Allow 5 minutes for this. Then ask for two volunteers to reorganize the notes on the sheets by collecting priorities that are the same or similar and placing them together. (For example, all notes that say "fundraising" would go together.) Then have them count the number that are the same and establish a "top five"—the five goals or goal categories that have the majority of notes will be group's five priorities. Allow 5 minutes for the volunteers to organize the notes and count up the totals. Remove the remaining sticky notes and write each of the five goals on its own sheet of newsprint hanging on the wall. Continue with the remainder of the activity.

After the large group has identified the five priority areas, divide the group into five smaller teams of three to five people. Assign each small group a working area in the room and give them the sheet of newsprint from the wall that corresponds to the priority they're going to focus on. Pass out at least one pad of self-adhesive notes and a pen or pencil to each group. Explain the small groups' responsibilities, referring to the posted information from "What Are Action Steps?":

Each team will now brainstorm ideas for specific action steps the large group can undertake to reach the goal on your sheet of newsprint. Write each idea on a separate note and stick the notes to the newsprint. When your small group is done, hang your sheet of newsprint with the sticky notes attached back on the wall.

Examples of action steps for a student council's goal of improved public relations might include the following (this is not an exhaustive list):

- Create a public relations committee.
- Volunteer to help with a public event such as a parade or carnival.
- Create a slogan that states the council's main priority.

Examples of action steps for a youth advisory board's goal to recruit new members might include the following (this is not an exhaustive list):

- Contact advisory boards in other communities for ideas.
- Create posters and hang them around the school.
- Have an all-school assembly.

Allow 10–15 minutes for small groups to complete the action steps related to their priority area and to hang the newsprint sheets back on the wall. Then invite a volunteer from each small group to explain the action steps identified by their team, allowing 3–5 minutes per group. When they've finished, say:

You have all come up with a lot of great action steps. Are there any that might work better for one of the other goals? Do you feel that any aren't realistic or reasonable?

Use 5–10 minutes to discuss the placement of the action steps and to move sticky notes around as the group deems necessary. If some steps are not realistic, remove those notes. A great deal of bantering and discussion can take place at this time. Stay alert to keeping the group on task and moving forward to narrow down the action steps for each area. If the teen leader of the group is facilitating this process, you may need to step in to help keep the group focused and to allow the youth leader to participate in the discussion.

Wrapping Up

After identifying and narrowing the action steps, keep each sheet of newsprint with its sticky notes intact. Arrange for yourself, a teen leader, or a reliable volunteer to collect and type up the goals and action steps. Distribute these to everyone in the group at the next meeting. Keep the large newsprint sheets to post during subsequent meetings.

Extending the Learning

Follow through on action steps. At the next group meeting, work with the group to determine assignments for specific action steps. For steps that require a committee to be developed, you may want to use the self-adhesive notes to facilitate this. For example, hang up newsprint with each committee or goal listed and allow teens to place a sticky note on the sheet that represents the area they want to work on. The same approach can be used for assigning specific action steps to group members: create a master list with all of the action steps and allow teens to post a note with their name on it next to the steps they want to be responsible for.

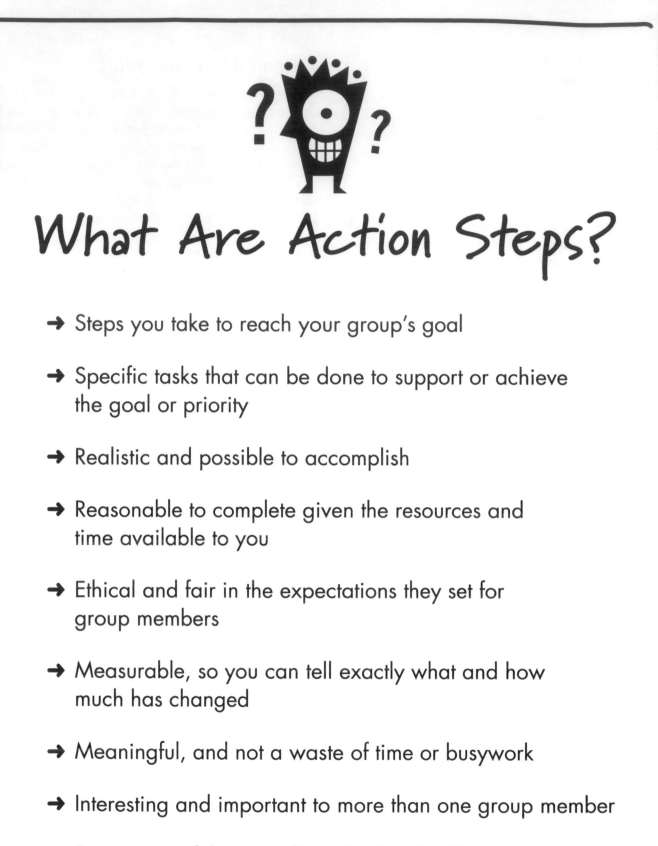

What Are Action Steps?

→ Steps you take to reach your group's goal

→ Specific tasks that can be done to support or achieve the goal or priority

→ Realistic and possible to accomplish

→ Reasonable to complete given the resources and time available to you

→ Ethical and fair in the expectations they set for group members

→ Measurable, so you can tell exactly what and how much has changed

→ Meaningful, and not a waste of time or busywork

→ Interesting and important to more than one group member

→ Supportive of the overall goals identified by your group

From *Teambuilding with Teens: Activities for Leadership, Decision Making, and Group Success* by Mariam G. MacGregor, M.S., copyright © 2008. Free Spirit Publishing Inc., Minneapolis, MN; www.freespirit.com. This page may be photocopied for individual, classroom, and group work only. For all other uses, call 800-735-7323.

The Million-Dollar Award

- Balancing personal and group values • Decision making
- Teamwork and group dynamics • Understanding social issues

(35–45 MINUTES)

This activity challenges teens to balance their personal values and choices with those of the group as they try to unanimously determine who should be awarded a million-dollar grant. To begin, participants rank the possible recipients independently. After they share their rankings with everyone, the entire group must come to agreement about the actual recipient of the grant. Learning to make decisions using consensus rule takes practice because majority vote is easier and brings groups to an end result more quickly. The process of arriving at consensus creates an in-depth learning experience and meaningful outcome. As can be expected, the discussions can get energetic as teens try to advocate for their preferred award recipient.

GOALS

Participants will:

- learn how to arrive at a group decision using consensus rule
- gain greater understanding of how personal and group values can conflict
- strengthen skills for working with others

MATERIALS NEEDED

- Pen or pencil for each participant
- Handout: "Profiles of Potential Award Winners" (pages 165–166)

GETTING READY

Make a copy of the "Profiles of Potential Award Winners" for each teen. Organize the room so teens will have a central location where they'll be able to discuss and debate who should receive the grant.

Setting the Stage

This activity touches on a number of issues related to human behavior and decision making. Most obvious are the first impressions individuals have of the prospective recipients profiled on the handout. Though participants may not be able to pinpoint the nature of their instant reactions to the descriptions, prejudices and biases come into play whether teens are aware of them or not. Discussing these first impressions during "Talk About It" can be useful and often warrants a follow-up activity addressing tolerance, diversity, and understanding prejudice.

Connected to these first reactions are the values upon which individuals base their choices and decisions. As with acknowledging prejudice or bias, time spent discussing the role and impact of values is important. Other activities addressing values, especially as they relate to leaders making decisions and balancing personal desires with the needs of a group, are worthwhile to conduct either before or after this activity. Consider these definitions to frame the activity discussions:

Bias: A bias is a preference for one thing over another. A bias isn't necessarily a negative factor in a decision, except when it works against one group or person over another group or person.

Prejudice: A prejudice is an opinion a person holds despite facts that indicate otherwise. A prejudice may also be a preconceived idea, usually unfavorable, that a person uses to make decisions or choices.

Values: These are the things (people, beliefs, places, etc.) that people find personally important and meaningful.

If teens in your group have little experience with consensus, it's worthwhile to conduct a brief discussion on the differences between consensus rule and majority rule. Consider these definitions to frame the activity and subsequent discussions:

Majority rule: Majority rule means the majority decides. Each person gets a vote, but the majority—greater than 50 percent of the members of the group—wins. Majority rule offers a way to make decisions quickly without spending a lot of time debating.

Consensus rule: This is a way for a group to make a decision without voting. With consensus rule, each person gets to voice his or her opinion, and then people discuss and compromise in order to arrive at a choice everyone can agree to. Consensus rule can be complicated and time consuming, but it is worthwhile when a group believes it's important for everyone to agree about a decision.

For this activity, the emphasis is on having the group reach consensus, therefore requiring some time to be spent talking about consensus rule, how it works, and when and why it's appropriate to use. Equally important is exploring when and why majority rule isn't appropriate—which is typically when consensus rule *is* a more effective approach. There are a number of factors that point to a group using consensus rule to reach a decision. It is most effective when:

- A leader realizes that if everyone doesn't agree on the same outcome, the decision won't be successful or people will try to get around it.

- The time available to make the decision is unlimited, as long as everyone agrees with the final choice.

- Power in the group is unevenly distributed and cliques could easily sway a decision if determined only by having everyone vote.

- Group members feel strongly about conflicting issues and believe a vote would minimize the importance of certain issues.

Of course, for purposes of this activity, a time frame for reaching consensus is imposed. In the hypothetical situation the activity presents, consensus rule is part of the process because of the diversity of the potential recipients and because it provides an opportunity to reinforce skills in decision making, compromise, and working with others. Suggestions for additional activities addressing consensus and majority rule, values, tolerance, and prejudice are included in "Extending the Learning."

Activity

Before passing out the profiles, introduce the activity and set the scene. You might say:

> Today, you are to consider yourselves members of a board of directors for an organization that will be giving one deserving person a one-million-dollar award. This award is a *grant*, which means the person who receives it will never have to pay it back. Having received it, the person can use it in any way she or he thinks is appropriate, as long as it fits the purpose for which the grant was given. All of the possible award recipients submitted applications explaining how they would use the money. Your board will monitor this, but for the most part will leave it up to the person receiving the money to be truthful and honest regarding how the grant is used.
>
> There are a few rules to guide your decision. First, the money can be given to only one person. You can't divide it among the candidates. Also, everyone on your board has to agree with the final decision. In other words, your decision will be reached by consensus. Who can tell me what consensus means?

Ask teens for their definitions and understanding of consensus, and if necessary, clarify their understanding of the term. When everyone understands and agrees to what it means, continue:

> Since you all understand what consensus is, you know that it means you cannot reach the final decision using a vote, unless you're using a simple vote to determine if the team has reached total agreement. All of you must do your best to advocate for the person you really want to receive the award. I am going to pass out profiles of the candidates—descriptions of who they are and how they want to use the grant. The first step will be for you to work individually to rank each candidate, giving the person you feel *most* deserves the award number 1 and the person you feel *least* deserves it number 10. Once you've ranked the candidates, wait quietly. Don't share your results with anyone until I tell you to do so. You have 5 minutes to do this. Any questions?

Pass out the profiles and allow 5 minutes for teens to complete their individual rankings. When everyone is done, proceed by saying:

> Now that you all have your preferred rankings, you'll go around the circle and each of you will read your ranked list for the rest of the group. At this point you don't need to explain your choices, because the group will begin discussing the reasons in a few minutes. The rest of you may want to make a checkmark on your sheets when you hear a ranking similar to yours. This will help when you start trying to decide on the final award winner.

Take 5 minutes to go around the circle and have everyone share their list. Then continue:

> Now that you've heard everyone's rankings, work as a team to select *one* individual to receive the million-dollar award. Again, the final decision will be made by consensus—everyone has to agree. Before you're done, select a spokesperson for your board who will announce who you chose and why. You have 25 minutes to make a group decision. I'll keep track of time and give you periodic updates.

At the end of 25 minutes, have the group wrap up debate and invite the spokesperson to present the candidate they decided on as the recipient of the grant. Ask the spokesperson to explain why the group selected the person. If the group was unable to choose a recipient, allow them to express frustration and offer opinions about why they couldn't reach agreement in addition to talking about the other aspects of the activity. Then move on to the "Talk About It" discussion.

Talk About It

After acknowledging to the group how difficult consensus can be, use 10 minutes to process the activity with questions like the following:

- When you read the profiles, did you have any instant reactions to some of the possible recipients? How did these prejudices or biases affect the individual choices you first made? How are your prejudices and biases connected to your values? Are you comfortable sharing your instant reactions? Why or why not?

- What did you learn about others in your group in terms of values and prejudices? How did these values or prejudices influence people's decision making?

- What if your group had been able to use majority rule? Would the outcome have been different? In what ways? Would you have been equally satisfied with the person selected? Explain.

- Do you feel you did a good job representing your values and interests in trying to get the recipient of your choice selected? Explain.

- In what ways does this activity reflect what takes place in real life when a group attempts to make a decision everyone can agree to? If your group were making a similar decision in the future, what would need to change so the process would be as productive and focused as possible?

Wrapping Up

Encourage teens to write their thoughts about the selection process and about issues that arose during the activity in their journals or notebooks. If time allows, have teens discuss how they would communicate the result to all the applicants.

Extending the Learning

Consider other types of awards. At another time, have teens discuss or design the requirements they would put into place for selecting scholarship recipients or granting other teen-related awards.

In this book, conduct the "Values Line" activity (pages 35–38) to delve deeper into personal values and "Choosing Sides" (pages 128–131) to further explore respecting different points of view.

Profiles of Potential Award Winners

Rank   **Profile**

_____   **Angela** is a 24-year-old single mother who lives in a large city. She wants to use the grant money to go back to school and start an organization that can help other mothers like herself. Some of the money would go to starting a childcare center so single moms could finish their schooling and get job training.

_____   **Jamie** is a seven-year-old girl who has suffered from bone cancer since she was three. Her family lives on a small working farm that struggles to compete with bigger farms. Jamie will die unless she receives new and expensive life-changing procedures, and the family would use some of the grant money (which would be awarded in Jamie's name but managed by her parents) to pay for these. They would also like to use some money for a family vacation to Disneyland. They will donate any remaining money to a cancer research fund.

_____   **John** is a 25-year-old former gang leader who became disabled when he was caught in a drive-by shooting while he was still involved in gangs. He started and runs a school that educates physically disabled youth. He will use the grant money to improve the school's facilities, increase its services, and hire additional staff for the students.

_____   **Simone** is a 30-year-old successful real estate developer. She'll use the money to become a partner in real estate deals that will return 10 times what she and her partners invest within five years. She plans to use half of her personal profits to build a modern housing project for senior citizens and will move her parents into the housing project when they are older.

_____   **Alex** is a 21-year-old who has paraplegia—the lower half of his body is paralyzed. He received his injuries during the Iraqi War and returned to his country after serving six months in the military. Although his condition qualifies him for disability benefits, Alex refuses to accept them. Alex will use the award money to help other young soldiers injured in war lead more normal lives and to improve services to homeless veterans on the streets or in shelters.

_____   **José** is an 18-year-old college student majoring in sociology. His parents died when he was 16. He hopes to use his college degree to address hunger and health problems in underdeveloped countries. He supports himself and his two younger sisters by taking odd jobs. José would use the grant money to take care of his family and pay for his education.

_____   **Mickey** is a 26-year-old waiter and recovering drug addict. He has been diagnosed with AIDS. He doesn't have medical insurance and has used all of his financial resources. His parents sold their home so he could get the medicine he needs to stay alive but the money is quickly running out. He will use the money to pay for his medical expenses with any remaining going to AIDS research.

MORE

From *Teambuilding with Teens: Activities for Leadership, Decision Making, and Group Success* by Mariam G. MacGregor, M.S., copyright © 2008. Free Spirit Publishing Inc., Minneapolis, MN; www.freespirit.com. This page may be photocopied for individual, classroom, and group work only. For all other uses, call 800-735-7323.

Rank	Profile

_____   **Stacie** is a 20-year-old struggling artist who grew up in a wealthy family. She refuses to use her family's money to further her career. She would use the award to lease or build space and purchase materials that would enable her and a group of other aspiring artists to have the security they need to develop and show their work. She would also create a foundation to support arts in schools where art budgets have been cut.

_____   **Victoria** is a six-month-old, developmentally disabled baby whose parents were killed in a car accident. Her grandparents have adopted her and want to move her to their native country. They would use Victoria's grant money to raise her and provide for her special needs. Any remainder would be put in a trust and awarded to Victoria on her 21st birthday.

_____   **Jim** is a 50-year-old businessman who is the chief executive officer of a large company and founder of the Needy Children's Scholarship Fund. He would use the grant money to send disadvantaged minority youth to college. Even though Jim went to jail for five years for selling company stock illegally, his personal net worth is now more than one billion dollars. For each of the past ten years, he has donated one million dollars to worthy causes.

From *Teambuilding with Teens: Activities for Leadership, Decision Making, and Group Success* by Mariam G. MacGregor, M.S., copyright © 2008. Free Spirit Publishing Inc., Minneapolis, MN; www.freespirit.com. This page may be photocopied for individual, classroom, and group work only. For all other uses, call 800-735-7323.

Closure

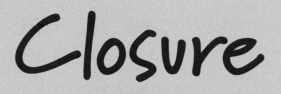

Back/Feedback

Letter to Myself

Back/Feedback

LEARNING CONCEPTS

- Appreciating others • Group closure
- Positive group dynamics

(20–30 MINUTES)

This closing activity provides teens the opportunity to give others in their group messages of appreciation. Pieces of construction paper are taped to participants' backs and everyone writes brief notes on each other's sheets. There is time for teens to privately read people's comments and acknowledge each other if desired.

GOALS

Participants will:

- provide positive feedback and appreciative comments to others
- bring the group experience to a meaningful close
- recognize one another for contributions made to the group

MATERIALS NEEDED

- Sturdy drawing paper or construction paper
- Markers that won't puncture or bleed through the paper, one or more for each participant
- Masking tape
- *Optional*—Newsprint (see "Variation")

Activity

Ask teens to select a piece of paper and one or more markers and write their name at the top of their papers. With the help of other group members, have participants tape their sheets of paper to their backs. Once everyone is prepared, begin the activity by saying:

The paper on your back is a place for your fellow group members to write a note of thanks, mention something they've learned from you, or offer other appreciative words about what you've brought to the group. You will do the same on their papers. You can move around as you wish in order to write on everyone's back. Please keep your messages positive and honest; avoid jokes or insider comments. You don't have to write a lot, but you want your messages to be meaningful and memorable. If you are comfortable doing so, sign your name so people know who wrote the note. Write at least one thing on every person's paper.

Allow 10–15 minutes for teens to walk around and write on everyone's paper. You'll want to move about the room as well, making sure people aren't overlooked and keeping the process moving. Ask participants to leave the papers on their backs until everyone is done writing on each person's sheet.

Then bring the group back together to remove their sheets at the same time. You may choose to have group members find private space or sit in a circle while they read their messages.

VARIATION

Some groups prefer to write on larger sheets of paper and a more stable surface. In this case, have teens tape individual sheets of newsprint to the wall and write their name at the top large enough so others can easily read it. Then have participants move from sheet to sheet writing messages of support and appreciation. Make sure that everyone writes on everyone else's sheet and that students don't read their own sheets until the entire rotation is complete.

Talk About It

Bring everyone together and take 5–10 minutes to have participants share their thoughts about being part of the group. Pay attention to include everyone in the group and make sure each member is recognized during the final discussion. Consider these discussion questions related to your group's experience:

- **Does anyone want to acknowledge specific comments someone else wrote to you?**

- **Overall, what would you say about your experience as part of this group?**

Wrapping Up

If you have access to a laminating machine, you may offer to laminate the back/feedback papers prior to teens' taking them home. You can also make reduced copies of the sheets so teens can use them as bookmarks for a regular reminder of what others appreciate about them. Otherwise, encourage teens to hang their sheets on a mirror or other visible place in their homes.

Letter to Myself

- Group closure or warm-up • Setting goals and creating vision

(20–25 MINUTES)

Less a group exercise than an opportunity for personal reflection, this activity can be used either at the closing group meeting to help teens focus on next steps or at an early meeting to encourage participants to set goals for personal growth within the group. Teens write letters to themselves, seal the letters in envelopes, and give them to you for safekeeping. At a later date, you will return the letters to teens by mail or in person. You will need enough space so all participants can reflect and write privately.

GOALS

Participants will:

- take time to reflect and document personal thoughts for future review
- set goals and vision
- experience meaningful group closure

MATERIALS NEEDED

- Writing paper (plain or fancy—a variety of types of paper can be nice for this activity)
- Pen or fine-point marker for each participant
- Business-size envelopes
- Large, sturdy rubber band
- Self-stick note
- First-class stamps (needed at a later date if you will be mailing the letters to teens)

GETTING READY

Determine when you will send the letters back to teens. If you're using the activity for closure, you may want to plan to have teens think of what they want to be doing one year from the day they write the letter. If you are using it as an opening activity, consider having them write letters they'll receive at the end of the group's time together (such as the close of the academic term, the end of camp, or the completion of weeks- or months-long service project).

170

If you will not be mailing the letters but plan to hand them out personally at a later meeting, determine when you'll do that based on the group's schedule. When that day arrives, you will want to set aside private time for teens to receive, read, and share thoughts about the letters as they relate to the group experience.

Setting the Stage

Since the content of the letters will be private, group discussion is not a necessary component of the activity. You may, however, want to build in some time for group sharing at the end of the meeting. The point of this discussion won't be to share details of the letters but rather to talk about general reflections on the group experience. For such discussion, plan a bit of time at the end of the meeting, but don't mention it as you set up the writing activity. This is to ensure that teens, who may be writing very private thoughts, will be able to fully focus on the personal writing task.

Activity

If using the activity for closure, begin by briefly summarizing your observations of teens' growth or development during their participation in the group. If using the activity as an opener, briefly describe what the group will be doing together and express your hope that the time will be a growing experience.

Then ask teens to select a piece of paper to use as stationery and to find a place in the room where they'll be comfortable writing privately. Pass out an envelope and pen or marker to each participant. Say:

Today you're going to write a letter to a very special person—you!

Instruct teens to write their names and complete addresses with postal code (or just their names, if you will be returning the letters in person) on the envelope. Have them determine the best address for reaching them one year from today (or another time period you've established). Students who are moving or anticipate changing addresses can use another reliable address, such as a grandparent or friend. In this case, make sure they use their own name as recipient and address it in care of (c/o) the other person. Then explain the letter writing and time frame as appropriate:

In your letter to yourself, write about where you see yourself (one year from today). Put today's date at the top. Write whatever nickname or special name you use for yourself. As you write to yourself, think about reading the letter in the future. You may want to write about certain goals and expectations you have. Or if you're dealing with a difficult situation right now, maybe you'll want to describe what's happening so you can check in with yourself about it. Whatever you write about, don't just write "Hi, what's up?" These letters are private. I won't read them. In fact, once you've finished your letter, seal it in your envelope and hand it to me. I will mail it to you (one year from today).

You can take some time to reflect on what you want to write before starting or think about it as you write. You have 15–20 minutes to write your letter. Enjoy it. I will collect the letters when time is up.

Answer any questions and then allow teens to write. You may want to walk around the room to keep people on task or to answer questions privately. When everyone is done, collect the sealed envelopes and write your return address in the upper lefthand corner of each. Wrap a rubber band around them and keep them in a safe place until you are due to mail them. Mark your calendar and put a sticky note on top of the stack indicating the date you need to mail the letters. With your return address on the letters, those that don't make it to the intended recipients will be returned to you so you can attempt to reach the individuals in another way.

Talk About It

If you'd like to allow time for sharing or to bring closure to the group, consider posing these broad-based questions:

- **Does anyone want to talk about any specific goals or vision you have expressed in your letter?**

- **Overall, what has your experience as part of this group taught you about yourself? (Overall, what do you hope to learn and experience as part of this group?)**

Wrapping Up

Take a few minutes to thank teens for their teamwork and efforts, and express your hopes and vision for them, as individuals and as a group.

Additional Resources

What You Need to Conduct the Activities

Tips for Teens: Facilitating Group Activities

Overview of Learning Concepts and Activities

Correlations with *Building Everyday Leadership in All Teens* Curriculum

What You Need to Conduct the Activities

Collect these items in a box or an easily accessible spot so you have a ready-to-use supply kit for group meetings. Before conducting any activity, make sure to review its "Materials Needed" list for additional items (such as perishables) that may be required.

Paper

Banner paper

Card stock (8½" x 11")

Colored paper (8½" x 11")

Construction paper (9" x 12")

Copier paper (8½" x 11" and 11" x 22")

Drawing paper (9" x 12" or 12" x 18")

Envelopes (standard-size, business-size, and document-size)

Newsprint or flip-chart pad

Poster board (heavier than newsprint)

White paper (8½" x 11")

General Supplies

Chalk

Colored pencils

Crayons

Duct tape

Markers

Masking tape

Pencils

Pens

Scissors

Stapler

Tape (clear, ¾" or 1")

Other Items

Balloons

Cloth strips or bandanas

Index cards (3" x 5")

Playing cards

Resealable plastic sandwich bags

Rubber bands

Safety pins

Self-adhesive note pads

Shoe box

String or yarn

Toothpicks (standard and multicolored)

From *Teambuilding with Teens: Activities for Leadership, Decision Making, and Group Success* by Mariam G. MacGregor, M.S., copyright © 2008. Free Spirit Publishing Inc., Minneapolis, MN; www.freespirit.com. This page may be photocopied for individual, classroom, and group work only. For all other uses, call 800-735-7323.

Tips for Teens: Facilitating Group Activities

As a teen leader, you may be called upon to facilitate activities for peers or younger students. Maybe you serve as a student council leader, camp counselor, peer mentor, youth assistant in a faith community, student coach, or in another leadership role. Whatever the setting, your audience—the group participants—will not only be following your direction, but also be learning from the way you communicate and present yourself. Here are a few tips to keep in mind as you step up to lead:

Before the Group Meets

Be prepared. Know where you are going and who will be in the group you're leading. If you'll be co-facilitating, make sure you've met with the other leader at least once before your visit.

Choose activities that fit the group. Consider the age and attention span of the group participants when choosing what activities to lead.

Familiarize yourself with each activity you will conduct. Read through the entire activity so you're familiar with everything necessary to conduct it smoothly. Gather and prepare any supplies you will need.

Seek tips from another leader. If you're working with someone who has already conducted the same activity, ask for any suggestions or strategies the person found helpful.

Practice. The more you practice, the greater your confidence will be when leading others. With this in mind, rehearse in front of a mirror or with a group of other teen leaders who will also be facilitating activities.

Dress appropriately. Remember, when you lead a group, you serve as a role model. It's important to show respect to the group you're guiding, as well as to the organization you represent, through the clothes you wear. You don't need to dress up, but you do want to wear comfortable clothes that are clean and appropriate. Dressing suitably will make

you feel more confident. When wearing a T-shirt, choose one without a message (unless it has the group's name or logo); this allows everyone to concentrate on the activity. You'll also want to remember to take off your hat and throw away your gum.

Eat something. Your focus will improve, as will your ability to deal with unexpected situations, if you've eaten something before the meeting. Snacks and drinks with caffeine or sugar can make you nervous, jittery, or even tired, so stick with more healthful choices. Avoid bringing food into the room, but do bring along some water—it will be useful if you start coughing or need to take a quick break to regroup or consider what a group participant has asked.

During the Activity

Lead with the audience in mind. If you're working with younger kids, think like them! The younger they are, the more excited they'll be to have you there. Kids who are older may act disinterested, but a leader's sincere enthusiasm usually brings a group around. Peers (including friends who may be in the group) might try their hardest to make your experience difficult. If this happens, take a moment to acknowledge what they're doing and ask them to participate in the activity as if someone other than you were guiding them. Avoid acting discouraged or defensive. If necessary, seek the assistance of a trusted adult to get the group focused on the activity.

From *Teambuilding with Teens: Activities for Leadership, Decision Making, and Group Success* by Mariam G. MacGregor, M.S., copyright © 2008. Free Spirit Publishing Inc., Minneapolis, MN; www.freespirit.com. This page may be photocopied for individual, classroom, and group work only. For all other uses, call 800-735-7323.

MORE ▶

Keep it lively. You don't need to do a song and dance, but any group likes to have the lessons keep moving. If you find yourself slowing down or getting confused, take a moment to get back on track. For example, you might ask for volunteers to list three things they've heard up to this point that really stand out, or you can have the group quickly brainstorm something related to the topic. This will give you a chance to clear your head and reconnect with where you were in the activity process.

Focus on strong communication skills. What you say, and how you say it, has a major impact on your success as a leader. Speak clearly, with a tone that shows you're involved and leaves everyone in the group feeling respected. Nonverbal messages—such as your posture, where you stand, and the way you use your hands—also say a lot. Looking at your audience and maintaining eye contact keeps you connected and helps hold people's interest. Pay attention, too, to what your facial expressions might be telling listeners. Your face and body speak volumes before you even say a word!

Listen to what others have to say. Nod, smile, and ask questions to learn more. Avoid arguing with or putting down anyone in the group. This takes time and energy from you and from the others who are trying to learn the leadership lessons you're guiding. If you need to move on, summarize and acknowledge what the person said: "I understand that you disagree. Let's hear what others think."

Ask for help if you need it. If you have trouble dealing with someone, ask the adult in the room to help. In most cases, the group's time is limited, and you don't want to spend valuable minutes taking care of problems. Remember to focus on the positive and involve everyone in the discussion by offering attention and appreciation equally.

Know that manners matter. Overall thoughtfulness and courtesy go a long way toward ensuring your success as a group leader. So do culturally appropriate language and sensitivity to people's feelings. Adult or peers observing you, such as teachers, parents, or other teen leaders, will be impressed and respect you for your leadership.

Request feedback. When you're done, ask for feedback from those who can give it best—the participants. Learning what others liked about the way you led the activity, and what could be improved, allows you to continue to gain confidence and skill as a leader and facilitator.

Find Out More

To learn more about communication and group leadership, check out these resources:

Are You Really Listening? Keys to Successful Communication by Paul J. Donoghue and Mary E. Siegel (Notre Dame, IN: Sorin Books, 2005). This book teaches you how to improve listening, pay attention, and be heard.

The Student Leadership Practices Inventory and Student Leadership Planner: An Action Guide to Achieving Your Personal Best by James M. Kouzes, Ph.D., and Barry Z. Posner, Ph.D. (San Francisco: Jossey-Bass, 2005). Use the inventory to measure your leadership behaviors in five areas and the planner to make improvements.

From *Teambuilding with Teens: Activities for Leadership, Decision Making, and Group Success* by Mariam G. MacGregor, M.S., copyright © 2008. Free Spirit Publishing Inc., Minneapolis, MN; www.freespirit.com. This page may be photocopied for individual, classroom, and group work only. For all other uses, call 800-735-7323.

Overview of Learning Concepts and Activities

Learning Concepts	Activities
Appreciating others	Back/Feedback
Awareness of social issues	Peace and Violence Webs
Balance and healthy life influences	Becoming My Best; My Whole Self
Balancing personal and group values	The Million-Dollar Award
Building trust	Traveling Teams
Communication skills	Bank Robbery; House of Cards; Human Shuffle; Puzzle; Snowflake; Teams Building; Traveling Teams; Treasure Hunt; The Web
Critical thinking and social change	Change the World; Peace and Violence Webs
Cultural perspectives on leadership	Wise Sayings
Dealing with cliques	Inside Out
Dealing with exclusion	Inside Out
Decision making	Campaign Teams; Challenges and Choices; The Million-Dollar Award; Post Your Plans
Developing a group project	Community Action Plan; Post Your Plans
Establishing group ground rules	Norms, Roles, and Expectations
Getting to know others	Change the World; Handprints; Martian Names; Our Community; Treasure Hunt
Group closure	Back/Feedback; Handprints; Letter to Myself
Group development	Body Map
Group warm-up	Handprints; Letter to Myself; Martian Names; The Party
Historical perspectives on leadership	Quote/End Quote
Including and accepting others	Inside Out
Inspiration and personal values	Quote/End Quote; Wise Sayings
Listening skills	Snowflake
Making a difference	Peace and Violence Webs; Power Trip
Meaning of leadership	Quote/End Quote; Wise Sayings
Moral independence	Smirk
Peer pressure, groupthink, and moral independence	Values Line
Personal values	Becoming My Best; Challenges and Choices; Choosing Sides; Handprints; Heroes; My Whole Self; Values Line

Overview of Learning Concepts and Activities (continued)

Learning Concepts	Activities
Personal values and diversity	Our Community
Positive group dynamics	Back/Feedback
Positive versus negative peer pressure	Smirk
Problem solving	Bank Robbery; Heroes; The Mole; Puzzle
Problem solving and working through crisis	The Web
Public speaking and presentation skills	Campaign Teams
Qualities of leadership	Campaign Teams; Heroes; Quote/End Quote; Treasure Hunt; Wise Sayings
Recognizing different points of view	Fruit Salad
Recognizing individual strengths of group members	The Party
Recognizing role models	Handprints; Heroes
Respecting different points of view	Choosing Sides
Self-awareness	Becoming My Best; Body Map; Choosing Sides; My Whole Self; Values Line
Setting and achieving a goal	House of Cards; Human Shuffle; Teams Building
Setting goals and creating vision	Community Action Plan; Letter to Myself; Post Your Plans
Sharing and communicating with others	Our Community
Teamwork and group dynamics	Bank Robbery; Campaign Teams; Community Action Plan; House of Cards; Human Shuffle; The Million-Dollar Award; The Mole; Norms, Roles, and Expectations; Post Your Plans; Puzzle; Smirk; Teams Building; Traveling Teams; Treasure Hunt; The Web
Trust and distrust	The Mole
Understanding ethics and ethical behavior	Challenges and Choices
Understanding the need for empathy and tolerance	Power Trip
Understanding others	Body Map; Norms, Roles, and Expectations; Our Community; The Party
Understanding and overcoming stereotypes	Fruit Salad
Understanding power	Power Trip
Understanding social issues	Choosing Sides; The Million-Dollar Award
Valuing individuality	Fruit Salad
Vision and values	Change the World

Correlations with *Building Everyday Leadership in All Teens Curriculum*

This chart shows the sessions in *Building Everyday Leadership in All Teens* that support or complement activities in *Teambuilding with Teens*.

Activities in *Teambuilding with Teens*	Sessions in *Building Everyday Leadership in All Teens*
Back/Feedback	3, 4, 5, 21
Bank Robbery	8, 13
Becoming My Best	4, 9, 18, 20
Body Map	9, 19, 20
Campaign Teams	3, 4, 14, 15, 16, 19
Challenges and Choices	9, 10
Change the World	9, 18
Choosing Sides	9, 10, 12
Community Action Plan	18
Fruit Salad	12, 18
Handprints	3, 4, 9
Heroes	2, 3, 4, 9, 18
House of Cards	5, 7
Human Shuffle	5, 8, 13
Inside Out	5, 7, 11, 12
Letter to Myself	9
Martian Names	1, 20
The Million-Dollar Award	6, 12, 15, 16
The Mole	5
My Whole Self	2, 3, 4, 9
Norms, Roles, and Expectations	7
Our Community	11, 12
The Party	3, 21
Peace and Violence Webs	18
Post Your Plans	13, 18, 20
Power Trip	6, 12
Puzzle	7
Quote/End Quote	2, 3, 4, 5, 9
Smirk	5
Snowflake	7, 8
Teams Building	7, 8, 14
Traveling Teams	17
Treasure Hunt	3, 8, 9, 11, 12
Values Line	9, 10, 17
The Web	5, 13, 14, 21
Wise Sayings	2, 3, 4, 5, 9

Correlations with Building Everyday Leadership in All Teens Curriculum

The chart shows the activities in *Teambuilding with Teens* that support or complement sessions in *Building Everyday Leadership in All Teens*.

Sessions in *Building Everyday Leadership in All Teens*	Activities in *Teambuilding with Teens*
1: Introducing Leadership	Martian Names
2: What Leadership Means to Me	My Whole Self; Quote/End Quote; Wise Sayings
3: The Leaders in My Life	Back/Feedback; Campaign Teams; Handprints; Heroes; My Whole Self; The Party; Quote/End Quote; Treasure Hunt; Wise Sayings
4: What I Look for in a Leader	Back/Feedback; Becoming My Best; Campaign Teams; Handprints; Heroes; My Whole Self; Quote/End Quote; Wise Sayings
5: Leaders and Followers	Back/Feedback; House of Cards; Human Shuffle; Inside Out; The Mole; Quote/End Quote; The Web; Wise Sayings
6: Power Play	The Million-Dollar Award; Power Trip
7: Communicate with Style	House of Cards; Inside Out; Norms, Roles, and Expectations; Puzzle; Snowflake; Teams Building
8: Hear, There, Everywhere: Active Listening	Bank Robbery; Human Shuffle; Snowflake; Teams Building; Treasure Hunt
9: My Values	Becoming My Best; Body Map; Challenges and Choices; Change the World; Choosing Sides; Handprints; Heroes; Letter to Myself; My Whole Self; Quote/End Quote; Treasure Hunt; Values Line; Wise Sayings

Sessions in *Building Everyday Leadership in All Teens*	Activities in *Teambuilding with Teens*
10: Doing the Right Thing	Challenges and Choices; Choosing Sides; Values Line
11: He Says, She Says	Inside Out; Our Community; Treasure Hunt
12: Choosing Tolerance	Choosing Sides; Fruit Salad; Inside Out; The Million-Dollar Award; Our Community; Power Trip; Treasure Hunt
13: Strength in Numbers	Bank Robbery; Human Shuffle; Post Your Plans; The Web
14: Turning Conflict into Cooperation	Campaign Teams; Teams Building; The Web
15: All in Favor, Say "Aye"	Campaign Teams; The Million-Dollar Award
16: All for One and One for All	Campaign Teams; The Million-Dollar Award
17: Taking Chances	Traveling Teams; Values Line
18: Thinking Creatively	Becoming My Best; Change the World; Fruit Salad; Heroes; Peace and Violence Webs; Post Your Plans
19: Having My Voice Heard	Body Map; Campaign Teams
20: Motivating the Team	Becoming My Best; Martian Names; Post Your Plans
21: Showing Appreciation, Celebrating Success	Back/Feedback; The Party; The Web

Index

A

The Abilene Paradox (film), 54
Abusive situations
  disclosure of, 5
  teen experiences with, 133
Acceptance of others, *see* Diversity;
    Tolerance
Accommodations for physical
    challenges
  Body Map, 16
  Choosing Sides, 128
  House of Cards, 46
  Human Shuffle, 49
  Smirk, 19
  Teams Building, 65
  Traveling Teams, 70
  Values Line, 35
Action plans, *see* Community Action
    Plan
Action steps, 158–160
Activities
  format, 2–3
  preparing for, 3, 174
  sequence, 2
  tips for teen facilitators, 174–175
Aesop's Fables, 151
All the King's Men (film), 84
Anti-Defamation League, 123
Appreciating others
  Back/Feedback, 168–169
  Body Map, 15–18
  Handprints, 12–13
  The Party, 98–99
  Treasure Hunt, 93–97
  see also Diversity; Feedback;
    Tolerance
*Are You Really Listening? Keys to
    Successful Communication*
    (Donoghue and Siegel), 175
Association for Challenge Course
    Technology, 54

B

Back/Feedback activity, 168–169
Balance, *see* Healthy life choices
Bank Robbery
  activity, 138–139
  clues handout, 140–141
  key, 142

Becoming My Best
  activity, 23–25
  handouts, 26, 27, 28, 29
Beliefs, *see* Values
Bias
  Campaign Teams, 82–84
  defined, 162
  The Million-Dollar Award, 161–164
  see also Stereotypes, overcoming
Body Map
  activity, 15–16
  questions handout, 17
  template handout, 18
The Book of Questions (Stock), 130
*Building Everyday Leadership in All
    Teens,* 178–180
Bullying
  Inside Out activity, 124–127
  teen experiences with, 133

C

Campaign Teams
  activity, 82–84
  candidate profile handouts, 85, 86,
    87, 88, 89
  resources, 84
Career preparation
  benefits of activities for, 1
  Challenges and Choices, 148–155
  Change the World (variation), 11
  Quote/Endquote, 100–104
The Carter Center, 136
Challenge by Choice (CbC) concept,
    70–71
Challenges and Choices
  activity, 148–150
  code of ethics handout, 155
  ethical choices inventory, 152–153
  inventory score summaries, 154
  resources, 150–151
Change the World icebreaker, 10–11
Children, *see* Younger children,
    adapting activities for
Choice Theory, 24
Choosing Sides
  activity, 128–130
  handout, 131
  resources, 130
Cliques, *see* Peer pressure

Closure activities
  Back/Feedback, 168–169
  Handprints, 12–13
  Letter to Myself, 170–171
Code of ethics, *see* Challenges and
    Choices
Communication skills
  Bank Robbery, 138–142
  House of Cards, 45–47
  Human Shuffle, 48–50
  messages, misinterpreting, 66, 67–68
  nonverbal communication, 45–47,
    77–79
  Our Community, 72–76
  Puzzle, 77–80
  Snowflake, 67–68
  Teams Building, 64–66
  tips for teen facilitators, 175
  Traveling Teams, 69–71
  Treasure Hunt, 93–97
  The Web, 55–62
Community Action Plan
  activity, 143–144
  handout, 145–147
Confidentiality, 4–5, 133
Confronting others
  The Mole, 51–54
  see also Group dynamics; Peer
    pressure
The Conscience of the Campus (Dillon
    and Davey), 151
Consensus rule, 162
*Counseling with Choice Theory: The New
    Reality Therapy* (Glasser), 24
Crisis, working through
  The Web activity, 55–62
  see also Emotional reactions
Critical thinking
  Change the World, 10–11
  Peace and Violence Webs, 132–136
Cultural perspectives
  Fruit Salad, 120–123
  Wise Sayings, 105–113
  see also Diversity

D

Decision making
Campaign Teams, 82–89
Challenges and Choices, 148–155
House of Cards, 45–47
The Million-Dollar Award, 161–166
Post Your Plans, 156–160
see also Problem solving
Difficult discussions, dealing with, 5, 57, 129
Disclosure of information, 5
Discrimination, see Bias; Stereotypes, overcoming
Distrust, see Trust and distrust
Diversity
Choosing Sides, 128–131
Fruit Salad, 120–123
Our Community, 72–76
see also Individuality; Tolerance; Understanding others

E

Elections activity, 82–89
Emotional reactions, 5, 57, 129
Empathy, understanding
Inside Out, 124–127
Power Trip, 115–119
see also Understanding others
Ethics
Challenges and Choices, 148–155
see also Values
Exclusion, dealing with
Inside Out, 124–127
see also Peer pressure
Expectation, defined, 41

F

Facilitators, see Teen facilitators
Family Education Web site, 123
Feedback
Back/Feedback, 168–169
defined, 41
Norms, Roles, and Expectations, 40–44
for teen facilitators, 5, 175
see also Appreciating others
Films, see Movies
"Foundation for a Better Life," 108
Free the Children, 136
Fruit Salad
activity, 120–123
resources, 123

G

Getting acquainted activities, see Icebreaker activities
Glasser, William, 24
Goals, setting and achieving
Community Action Plan, 143–147
House of Cards, 45–47
Human Shuffle, 48–50
importance of, 4
Letter to Myself, 170–171
The Mole, 51–55
Post Your Plans, 156–160
Teams Building, 64–66
Ground rules, establishing, 40–44
Group development activities
Body Map, 15–18
My Whole Self, 30–34
Norms, Roles, and Expectations, 40–44
Group dynamics
stages of, 3–4
see also Teamwork and group dynamics
Group guidelines
establishing, 4
Norms, Roles, and Expectations, 40–44
Group projects, developing
Community Action Plan, 143–147
Post Your Plans, 156–160
Groupthink
defined, 20
Smirk, 19–22
Values Line, 35–38
Guidelines, see Group guidelines

H

Handprints icebreaker, 12–13
Healthy life choices
Becoming My Personal Best, 23–29
My Whole Self, 30–34
Heroes activity, 90–92
Historical perspectives
Quote/End Quote, 100–104
see also Cultural perspectives
House of Cards activity, 45–47
Human Shuffle activity, 48–50
Humor, Smirk activity, 19–22

I

Icebreaker activities
Change the World, 10–11
Handprints, 12–13
Martian Names, 8–9
Our Community, 72–76
Treasure Hunt, 93–97
Idealist.org, 136
IF . . . Questions for Teens (McFarlane and Saywell), 130
Including others
Bank Robbery, 138–142
Inside Out, 124–127
see also Teamwork and group dynamics
Individuality
Body Map, 15–18
Fruit Salad, 120–123
My Whole Self, 30–34
Our Community, 72–76
The Party, 98–99
see also Appreciating others; Diversity
Inside Out
activity, 124–126
role-play scenarios, 126
Inspirational sayings
Quote/End Quote, 100–104
Wise Sayings, 105–113
Institute for Global Ethics, 151
Internet Movie Database, 136

J/K/L

Journals, see Writing activities
The Kids' Book of Questions (Stock), 130
"Laws of Life" essay context, 108
Leaders
quotes and proverbs about, 103, 109–110
selecting for activities, 5
tips for teen facilitators, 174–175
see also Role models
Leadership qualities
Campaign Teams, 82–89
Heroes, 90–92
The Party, 98–99
Quote/End Quote, 100–104
Treasure Hunt, 93–97
The Web, 55–62
Whole Leader, 31, 34
Wise Sayings, 105–113
Learning concepts overview, 176–177
Letter to Myself activity, 170–171

Listening skills
    Snowflake, 67–68
    tips for teen facilitators, 175
    see also Communication skills

M

Majority rule, 162
Making a difference
    Peace and Violence Webs, 132–136
    Power Trip, 115–119
    see also Social issues
"Making Ethical Decisions: The Basic
    Primer on Using the Six Pillars
    of Character to Make Better
    Decisions and a Better Life"
    (Josephson), 151
Martian Names icebreaker, 8–9
Materials list, 173
Media Awareness Network, 123
Messages, misinterpreting, 66, 67–68
The Million-Dollar Award
    activity, 161–164
    profiles of potential award winners,
        165–166
The Mole
    activity, 51–54
    instructions handouts, 55
Moral independence
    defined, 20
    Smirk activity, 19–22
    Values Line activity, 35–38
*More Would You Rather? Four Hundred
    and Sixty-Five More Provocative
    Questions to Get Teenagers Talking*
    (Fields), 130
Movies
    The Abilene Paradox, 54
    All the King's Men, 84
    Internet Movie Database, 136
    Teach with Movies, 151
My Whole Self
    activity, 30–32
    handout, 33
    Whole Leader handout, 34

N

Negative peer pressure, 20
Nonverbal communication
    House of Cards, 45–47
    Puzzle, 77–80
Norm, defined, 41

Norms, Roles, and Expectations
    activity, 40–42
    handout, 43–44
Notebooks, *see* Writing activities

O

Obstacle course, 69–71
101 Ethical Dilemmas (Cohen), 130
Opinions, expressing, 128–131
Our Community
    activity, 72–74
    handouts, 75, 76
Outsiders
    Inside Out, 124–127
    see also Peer pressure

P

The Party activity, 98–99
Peace and Violence Webs
    activity, 132–136
    resources, 136
PeaceJam, 136
Peer pressure
    Inside Out, 124–127
    Smirk, 19–22
    Values Line, 35–38
Peer pressure,
    Fruit Salad, 120–123
Personal reflection, *see* Reflection
Personal values, *see* Values
Political campaign activity, 82–89
Positive peer pressure, 20
Post Your Plans
    action steps, 160
    activity, 156–159
Power Trip
    activity, 115–117
    handouts, 118, 119
    resources, 117
Prejudice
    defined, 162
    see also Bias; Stereotypes, overcoming
Priorities, *see* Goals, setting and
    achieving
Problem solving
    Bank Robbery, 138–142
    Heroes, 90–92
    The Mole, 51–54
    Puzzle, 77–80
    The Web, 55–62
    see also Decision making
Professional Ropes Course Association,
    54
Project Adventure, 54, 70

Proverbs, 105–113
Public speaking activity, 82–89
Puzzle activity, 77–80

Q

*The Quality School: Managing Students
    Without Coercion* (Glasser), 24
Quote/End Quote
    activity, 100–102
    handouts, 103, 104

R

Reality Therapy, 24
Reality Therapy for the 21st Century
    (Wubbolding), 24
Recognition, *see* Appreciating others;
    Feedback
Reflection
    encouraging, 6
    Letter to Myself, 170–171
    see also Values
Right versus wrong debates, *see*
    Challenges and Choices
Role, defined, 41
Role models
    Becoming My Personal Best, 23–29
    Handprints, 12–13
    Heroes, 90–92
Role playing
    Inside Out, 124–127
    as teaching technique, 5
Ropes courses, 54

S

Self-awareness
    Becoming My Personal Best, 23–29
    Body Map, 15–18
    Choosing Sides, 128–131
    My Whole Self, 30–34
    Values Line, 35–38
Sharing with others
    Our Community, 72–76
    Treasure Hunt, 93–97
Simulation Training Systems, 117
Smirk activity, 19–22
Snowflake activity, 67–68
Social issues
    Change the World, 10–11
    Choosing Sides, 128–131
    Fruit Salad, 120–123
    Heroes, 90–92
    Inside Out, 124–127
    The Million-Dollar Award, 161–166
    Peace and Violence Webs, 132–136
    Power Trip, 115–119

Society of Professional Journalists, 151
Speeches, making, 82–89
StarPower, 117
Stereotypes, overcoming
    Campaign Teams, 82–89
    Fruit Salad, 120–123
    resources, 123
    see also Bias; Power Trip
Strengths, recognizing
    My Whole Self, 30–34
    The Party, 98–99
The Student Leadership Practices
    Inventory and Student Leadership
    Planner (Kouzes and Posner),
    175
Supplies list, 173

T

Teacher Vision Web site, 123
Teaching Tolerance organization, 123
Teach with Movies, 151
Teams Building activity, 64–66
Teamwork and group dynamics
    Back/Feedback, 168–169
    Bank Robbery, 138–142
    Campaign Teams, 82–89
    Community Action Plan, 143–147
    House of Cards, 45–47
    Human Shuffle, 48–50
    The Million-Dollar Award, 161–166
    The Mole, 51–54
    Norms, Roles, and Expectations,
        40–44
    Post Your Plans, 156–160
    Puzzle, 77–80
    Smirk, 19–22
    stages of group dynamics, 3–4
    Teams Building, 64–66
    Traveling Teams, 69–71
    Treasure Hunt, 93–97
    The Web, 55–62
Teen facilitators
    tips for, 174–175
    see also Younger children, adapting
        activities for
Teen Ink: What Matters (Meyer et al.),
    107
Teen Ink Web site, 108
They Broke the Law—You Be the Judge
    (Jacobs), 151

Tolerance
    Choosing Sides, 128–131
    emphasizing, 5
    Fruit Salad, 120–123
    group guidelines, 4
    Inside Out, 124–127
    The Million-Dollar Award (extending
        the activity), 164
    Power Trip, 115–119
    see also Diversity; Understanding
        others
Traveling Teams activity, 69–71
Treasure Hunt
    activity, 93–94
    questions handout, 95–96
    score sheet, 97
Trust and distrust
    The Mole, 51–54
    Traveling Teams, 69–71
Tuckman, Bruce W., 3

U

Understanding others
    Body Map, 15–18
    Norms, Roles, and Expectations,
        40–44
    Our Community, 72–76
    The Party, 98–99
    see also Diversity; Tolerance
Unhappy Teenagers: A Way for Parents
    and Teachers to Reach Them
    (Glasser), 24
University of San Diego Ethics
    Updates, 151

V

Values
    Becoming My Personal Best, 23–29
    Challenges and Choices, 148–155
    Change the World, 10–11
    Choosing Sides, 128–131
    defined, 162
    Fruit Salad, 120–123
    Handprints, 12–13
    Heroes, 90–92
    importance of, 36
    The Million-Dollar Award, 161–166
    moral independence, 20
    My Whole Self, 30–34
    Our Community, 72–76
    Quote/End Quote, 100–104
    Values Line, 35–38
    Wise Sayings, 105–113

Values Line
    activity, 35–37
    sample words handout, 38
Violence
    bullying, 124–127
    Peace and Violence Webs, 132–136
Vision, creating
    Change the World, 10–11
    Community Action Plan, 143–147
    Letter to Myself, 170–171
    Post Your Plans, 156–160
    The Web, 55–62
    see also Goals, setting and achieving

W

Warm-up activities, see Icebreaker
    activities
Warren, Robert Penn, 84
The Web
    activity, 56–58
    key words handout, 59–60
    statements handout, 61–62
What Would We Do If . . . (Bunker and
    Osborne), 151
What Would You Do? (Criswell), 151
Whole Leader activity, 31, 34
Wilderdom Peace and Experiential
    Education, 136
Wise Sayings
    activity, 105–108
    handouts, 109–110, 111–112
    key, 113
    resources, 107
Writing activities
    encouraging, 6
    Fruit Salad, 122
    Teams Building, 66
    Traveling Teams, 71
Writing from the Heart: Young People
    Share their Wisdom (Veljkovic
    and Schwartz), 107

Y

Younger children, adapting activities for
    Fruit Salad, 121
    Inside Out, 124
    The Party, 98–99
    Puzzle, 79
    Values Line, 37
    Values Line (variation), 37
    Wise Sayings, 106
Youth Service America (YSA), 136

ABOUT THE AUTHOR

Mariam G. MacGregor, M.S., founded and runs Youthleadership.com, an online clearing-house and resource center for individuals working with youth leaders. The Web site connects thousands of individuals around the world with information and links that can help create meaningful leadership opportunities for teens and young adults.

After working with college-age student leaders at Syracuse University in New York, Santa Clara University in California, and Metropolitan State College of Denver, Mariam served as school counselor and coordinator of leadership programs at Vantage Point Campus Alternative High School in Colorado. While there, she received Honorable Mention, "School Counselor of the Year," by the Colorado School Counselors Association in 1999.

Over the past 16 years, Mariam has consulted with various organizations, written articles on youth leadership for different publications, and presented workshops to diverse audiences emphasizing meaningful youth leadership experiences in schools and communities. In addition to *Teambuilding with Teens,* her curriculum *Building Everyday Leadership in All Teens* has also received the Distinguished Achievement Award from the Association of Educational Publishers (AEP). Mariam's leadership books and Youthleadership.com have been featured in the National Association for Secondary School Principals catalog, *Leadership for Student Activities* magazine (a monthly magazine for advisors who work with student councils and National Honor Society chapters), and the Canadian Association of Student Activity Advisors catalog and Web site, among others. She lives in the foothills outside Denver, Colorado, with her husband and children.

Other Great Books from Free Spirit

Building Everyday Leadership in All Teens
Promoting Attitudes and Actions for Respect and Success
by Mariam G. MacGregor, M.S., foreword by Barry Z. Posner, Ph.D.
Every teen can be a leader. That's because leadership is not just about taking the lead in big ways, but in everyday small things, too. The 21 sessions in this book help teens build leadership skills including decision-making, risk taking, team building, communication, creative thinking, and more. Requires use of the student book, *Everyday Leadership*. Reproducibles include assessment tools and exams. For teachers and youth workers, grades 6–12. *208 pp.; softcover; illust.; 8½" x 11"*

Everyday Leadership
Attitudes and Actions for Respect and Success
by Mariam G. MacGregor, M.S., foreword by Barry Z. Posner, Ph.D.
Written and experiential activities help teens develop a leadership attitude, discover their leadership potential, and build leadership skills. Created for use with *Building Everyday Leadership in All Teens,* this consumable guide also functions as a stand-alone resource for personal growth. For ages 12 & up. *144 pp.; lay-flat binding; 7" x 9"*

Everyday Leadership Cards
Writing and Discussion Prompts
by Mariam G. MacGregor, M.S.
This easy-to-use deck of discussion and writing prompts helps instill a leadership attitude in teens by encouraging them to think about their beliefs and goals, how they communicate, what they admire in a leader, and more. For ages 10 & up. *60 cards; 2-color; 3" x 4½"*

Everyday Leadership Skills & Attitude Inventory CD-ROM
And Other Tools for Teen Leadership Education
by Mariam G. MacGregor, M.S.
This field-tested youth leadership inventory is a great way to enhance and personalize any youth leadership development or character education program. Young people gain valuable insights into their strengths, beliefs, and tendencies as leaders and explore ways they can enhance them. For youth leaders, teachers, and counselors, grades 5 & up.

What Do You Stand For? For Teens
A Guide to Building Character
by Barbara A. Lewis
This book invites teens to explore and practice honesty, kindness, empathy, integrity, tolerance, patience, respect, and more. Includes inspiring quotations, thought-provoking dilemmas, meaningful activities, and true stories about real kids who exemplify positive character traits. Updated resources point the way toward character-building books, organizations, programs, and Web sites. For ages 11 & up. *288 pp.; softcover; B&W photos and illust.; 8½" x 11"*

The Kids' Guide to Working Out Conflicts
How to Keep Cool, Stay Safe, and Get Along
by Naomi Drew, M.A.
Proven ways to avoid conflict and defuse tough situations, written by an expert on conflict resolution and peacemaking. Includes tips and strategies for dealing with bullies, lessening stress, and more. For ages 10–14. *160 pp.; softcover; illust.; 7" x 9"*

Leader's Guide
Includes 25 reproducible handout masters. For teachers, grades 5–8.
112 pp.; softcover; lay-flat binding; 8½" x 11"

Interested in purchasing multiple quantities?
Contact edsales@freespirit.com or call 1.800.735.7323 and ask for Education Sales.

Many Free Spirit authors are available for speaking engagements, workshops, and keynotes.
Contact speakers@freespirit.com or call 1.800.735.7323.

For pricing information, to place an order, or to request a free catalog, contact:

Free Spirit Publishing Inc. • 217 Fifth Avenue North • Suite 200 • Minneapolis, MN 55401-1299
toll-free 800.735.7323 • local 612.338.2068 • fax 612.337.5050 • help4kids@freespirit.com • www.freespirit.com